I Heard a Meadowlark

Marion Bruce Eskelson

iUniverse, Inc.
New YorkBloomington

I Heard a Meadowlark

iUniverse books may be ordered through booksellers or by contacting:

iUniverse
1663 Liberty Drive
Bloomington, IN 47403
www.iuniverse.com
1-800-Authors (1-800-288-4677)

ISBN: 978-1-4401-7682-1 (pbk)
ISBN: 978-1-4401-7683-8 (ebook)

Printed in the United States of America

iUniverse rev. date: 12/2/09

In Appreciation

Industrialization and urbanization of the north Red River Valley have erased most landmarks of my childhood. Kane, Grandfather's great barn, the junior high I attended; all are gone. Yankton College has closed its doors. In writing my memoirs, I hope to record a way of life that no longer exists.

Barbara, infallible source of childhood events, chastised me after reading a draft of my manuscript. I reminded her these stories I told represented my memories. Unable to resolve these sisterly disagreements as to which of us had the most accurate childhood memories, we continued on down to the end of her road still best friends, beloved sisters.

If I named all those who participated in helping me tell my little history, the list would be longer than the story. Therefore, I thank the Amazing Writers Group and its stalwart facilitators, Joan Lindgren and Donna Boyle, for their patience, humor, and gentle advice.

A wise and witty group of writers further encouraged my efforts during Thursday luncheons at Nati's in Ocean Beach.

I have promised the Monday Breakfast Committee a copy of this book as payment for not letting me give up.

Denys Horgan provided me with the push I needed to continue my story.

Without Kennett Harrison and her intrepid advice, I would have preformed a ceremonial burning of these papers instead of breathing deeply and continuing.

And what would I have done without my darling family? *I am not going to read that story one more time for you,* they chorused.

What more could I ask?

Thank you, all of you.

For Joan

Table of Contents

Part 1:
Who's Who

Before Agribusiness consumed family farms; during the Great Depression and World War II; there lived an agrarian society in the valley of the Red River of the North. Exploiting the generosity of this valley of the North, farming formed the backbone of scattered hamlets, villages, towns and a major city or two.

My story begins in the Canadian portion of that great valley on September 10, 1929. My earliest memories, fragmented as are all recollections of childhood, consist of life on Grandfather's farm.

Grandfather went west seeking opportunities Ontario would never provide him. Taking his wife and two young children, he set out to build his own empire. Kane, Manitoba, Canada provided him such opportunity. In the early 1900's, he began to build his dream on the newly broken sod of the northern part of the Red River Valley. He brooked no nonsense on his newly plowed land. His stern Scots Presbyterianism housed in his 6 foot 4 inch frame allowed him neither to give quarter nor ask for any. He not only farmed a section and a half of this rich wheat land, he also bred and imported Shorthorn cattle and Clydesdale horses.

Grandmother, also from Ontario, had been schooled to be a gentleman's wife. Despite her diminutive stature, she accomplished her role in the cultural desert of a sparsely populated farming community. Her orderly

Baptist serenity, faith in the WCTU, and independent source of money provided security in the midst of crises.

Mother, youngest of Jim and Nora Davidson's two daughters, bravely bore the disgrace of having been deserted by her husband and the father of her three children. Her bi-polar illness provided gossip far more engrossing than anything any Ma Perkins soap opera could provide.

Douglas Anderson Bruce, my father, son of an immigrant family from Scotland, had been decorated by the British and Canadian military for service with Lord Strathcona's Light Horse Cavalry regiment during World War One. The ghost of his alcoholic absence lay in frozen silence over our lives.

Jim and Barbara, my older brother and sister, formed a tightly closed alliance that armed them against Grandfather's fury, the terror of Mother's mania, and her grinding depressions.

John Gunn, a native of Edinburgh, co-managed the farm with Grandmother during Grandfather's lengthy trips as representative of the Shorthorn Breeders Association and the Clydesdale Breeders Association. John's and Mother's love affair was the best kept open secret in the community of Kane.

In 1939 Canada joined forces with the rest of the British Commonwealth and declared war on the Axis. Mother moved us permanently to Rapid City, South Dakota. We soon adjusted to urban living in this town of a little more than eleven thousand people perched on the edge of the recently closed frontier. Auntie Edna, Mother's only sister, ran the Black Hills General Hospital with the same steely determination necessary for any successful pioneer woman. Auntie Edna exercised her control with the coolness of a professional gambler. She meted out her iron-clad will at a time when few women were allowed to write personal checks. Standing less than 5 feet tall, her ability to wield her authority equaled that of the powerful business and professional men whose position on the hospital board enabled her to govern an institution that met the highest of state standards.

At eighteen, I made my first attempt at escape by attending Yankton College, the first college in the Dakota Territories. Located in Yankton in the south-eastern corner of South Dakota on a bluff overlooking the Missouri River, this little beacon of academic light awarded me a degree in 1951.

After a dismal stint as case worker for the State Department of Child Welfare, I made my second try at escape by moving to Texas and into what would turn into a marriage that would last for almost fifty years.

My final escape led our little family to San Diego, California where we have lived ever since except for Richard who died on my birthday in 2000. But that escapade deserves a volume of its own.

In telling my tale, I hope to provide a glimpse into a way of life that now can only exist in memory.

Part 2:
In the Beginning 1929–1939

I wonder who my father is. No one ever speaks his name. I just know who he is not. He is not John Gunn, the Scotsman, who keeps the farm running smoothly and takes orders from Grandmother when Grandfather is not there, which is most of the time. I sit on John's lap while he reads Robert Burns to me. He laughs at Rab the Ranter and I laugh with him. He smells of tobacco and says Turret cigarettes any time I ask him. He has auburn hair and loves my mother. After the Nazis bomb Edinburgh, he joins the Royal Canadian Air Force. He is killed while on a training flight.

~ ~ ~

Seated beside Mother at the dining room table, unable to bear the heat and humidity, I remove my dress and carefully place it over the back of my high chair. Too hot I say into Mother's stricken face. Grandfather continues to carve and serve the roast, refusing to acknowledge my sacrilege.

~ ~ ~

Suzie comes to work for us. She hugs and kisses Jim and Barbara, cradles me in her arms, calls me her little Boodie. She never reveals the meaning of this special term, leaving me forever named with her mysterious endearment.

In the quiet of a winter night, Suzie's muffled sobs waken my mother. Finding Suzie gazing out at the moonlight's brilliant reflection off the white, frozen fields, Mother tries to comfort her. *It looks just like Russia, you know,* Suzie begins. *Did you ever hear a starving child cry? When the Bolsheviks came, they took all my family out of their beds and into the streets. Shot them all dead. They left me and Anya alive. We walked out of Russia.*

~ ~ ~

Mother is gone. I don't know where she is. Sometimes she and my grandfather go to Detroit to buy a new car from the factory. Grandfather buys a new car every year. He wears them out he says. Sometimes the car is worn out because it has been in a wreck. Sometimes Mother goes into Winnipeg for the day to shop and eat lunch and see a movie. Sometimes she is gone for just a little while. This time, she has been gone a long, long time. No one says where she is or when she will be back. I use a washcloth to muffle the sounds I make crying myself to sleep.

~ ~ ~

Stop that crying, the grown-ups tell me, *or I'll give you something to cry about.* Except Grandmother, she never says that. She never spanks. She just says shame-shame when I am naughty.

~ ~ ~

Jim and Barbara tire of playing with me. I am too little, too fat, too short of leg. I get in the way of their activities. To discourage me from hanging around, they take me behind the currant bushes. They tell me if I open my mouth and shut my eyes they will give me something to make me wise. When I cooperate, they stuff my mouth with mud and currants. I go to the house to play in the safer company of my dolls.

~ ~ ~

Barbara again sets up her beauty salon on the side porch. She has purloined a kerosene lamp, matches, a dishtowel, Mother's curling iron and mirror. I am the client. She swaddles me in the dishtowel and carefully lights the lamp. She skillfully heats the curling iron to red-hot over the kerosene lamp. My short, curly hair does not dissuade her. She deftly applies the curling iron to my hair, singeing it. Occasionally she burns my neck and ears. I weep silently. She tells me it doesn't hurt so convincingly that I believe her. She tidies everything up and puts all her equipment back where she found it. Our clandestine activities remain unobserved

~~~

Once again assigned the task of playing with me, Jim and Barbara take me out to the tire swing housed in the windbreak. Secured to a big tree with a stout rope, the tire hangs secluded in the windbreak.

Want to swing? they ask.

I happily climb into the tire. Jim and Barbara slowly twirl the tire around and around on its sturdy rope. My feet inch farther and farther away from the ground.

Hang on tight, Jim orders. He releases the tire. First the tire untwists rapidly in one direction, and then it begins its Newtonian progression until it stops.

I fall from the swing, retch into the dirt. Alarmed, they try to help me to my feet. I reel drunkenly, collapse in the dirt again. Eventually the nausea and dizziness subside.

After Jim recites *Tattletale Tit your tongue shall be split and all the dogs in town shall have a bit of it,* Barbara dusts me off, returns me to the house.

~~~

Alone in the kitchen with Mother, I stand beside her on a chair. She concentrates on her job of food preparation.

> *I'm tired of being the baby,* I complain.
> *Are you,* she asks absently.
> *I want you to have another baby,* I say.
> *Stop pestering,* she says crossly, dismissing me with a scowl.

~ ~ ~

Charlie Widden, a Sunday dinner guest, is the only adult I have ever met who is at my eye level. He fascinates me. He gets up on a dining room chair the same way I do, by standing on the chair rung, throwing one leg on the seat and pulling himself up. His head is bigger than mine. His feet don't work the same way mine do. I watch his every move. He dresses in a suit, shirt and tie. I am dressed in a smocked dress with matching panties and a large bow of taffeta ribbon on top of my head. I watch every bite he puts into his mouth. He drinks coffee. I am given a glass of milk. He joins in the conversation with the other adults. I do not. The dinner conversations, animated and lengthy, amuse the adults.

When we finally catch Grandfather's attention, he mercifully grants each child's request to be excused from the table. Jim, Barbara and I make a beeline to the windbreak and our carefully concealed stash. We smoke what is available; dried corn silk in summer, Indian weed in the fall, and filched tobacco from the tins the hired men store on top of one of the kitchen cupboards. We smoke and relax, happy to be relieved of the strain of being seen and not heard at the interminable dinner table.

Jim begins our favorite joke. *Knock, knock,* he says. *Who's there?* Barbara and I intone. *Charlie,* he says. *Charlie who?* we ask. Jim delivers the punch line. *Charlie Widden.* We laugh until our sides ache.

Long after we are grown, this joke will send us into fits of laughter.

~ ~ ~

The outhouse has been built to Grandmother's specifications. To clean it, a hired man hitches a horse to a container concealed at the bottom of the privy. Then the container is hauled to the manure pile where it is dumped. The hired man dusts the container with sweet lime, returns it to the outhouse. No offensive odors are ever emitted. The outhouse, tucked between the two rows of windbreak, provides a perfect spot for tree climbing. Jim and Barbara show me how to climb a tree to get up on the outhouse roof. After I have followed their directions, they jump off and run away. Afraid to jump, I wait and wait until Mother finds me to help me down.

~ ~ ~

Barbara owns one doll, a really fancy doll with real hair, a china face, arms, hands, and legs, whose eyes open and close. Her bonnet, dress, shoes, and socks are intact. Barbara never takes her out of the box, but admires her from afar. One day I abduct the doll, open the basement door, and throw her down the stairs. She smashes to pieces on the concrete floor. The crash brings everyone running. Barbara howls in outraged disbelief. Grandmother turns to me and says, *Shame-Shame.*

~ ~ ~

After Suzie leaves, Annie becomes the hired girl. She plays with us after she finishes with her chores, takes us out to the barn, plays hide and seek. It takes her a long time to find us if we decide to hide in one of the horse stalls. The Clydesdales stand patiently, ignoring our whispered giggles among their shaggy hooves. Annie helps us bundle up warmly to go sledding. She helps Jim hitch Fly, his black and white Shetland pony, to the pony-sized stoneboat. We pile on, Jim coaxes Fly into a gallop and her little hoovs throw snow back on us. Annie holds on to us, making sure we never fall off.

Annie quits working for us so she can marry Alex Wilkie, Old John Wilkie's son.

~ ~ ~

Tina replaces her. Annie was little and quick. Tina is large and slow. She never plays with us. We decide we don't like Tina.

~ ~ ~

Grandmother has purchased a new hearing aid. She has given Jim the old one to play with. He promptly takes it apart and hooks the battery and copper wires up to the doorknob of the door leading into Tina's room. From a hidden vantage point, he waits. When Tina grasps the doorknob, he flips the switch, giving Tina an unexpected jolt.

We take Mother's hairpins and carefully bend them in the middle. We place them, pointy side up, underneath the bottom sheet of Tina's bed. She plops into bed that night to find it uninhabitable. She would quit her job but her family depends on the money she sends them for their survival.

We climb up on a kitchen cabinet and softly chant: Tina is a cow's tail. She storms out of the room to find Mother and tell on us. Even a dreaded whipping cannot dissuade us from our games with Tina.

We follow Tina around while she is working. We mimic her every move until, unable to tolerate our teasing, she turns around and smacks one of us with a large, open, meaty hand. I am always the one closest to her. I am always the one who gets smacked. The game ends when everyone tires of my tears.

Your three children make life a hell on earth for me, Tina tells Mother.

~ ~ ~

Two stories are told about Grandfather. One; when he was sixteen he took the buggy whip away from his mother, telling her she would never beat him with it again. Two; he sold a bull for twenty-five hundred dollars at the Brandon Fair in 1909. He has been rich ever since.

~ ~ ~

Grandfather takes us out to one of the wheat fields. We are to pull out the wild mustard. The wheat is above my head. Coarse and rough, the green stalks grab at my clothes. Grandfather shows us how to pull out the weeds without disturbing the grain, how to shake the roots against our legs without wasting the soil, how to walk carefully without crushing the green wheat. I am drowning in the heat and humidity. I am scratched and itchy from the plants. The weeds have a choking smell. I fall on the ground, rolling, crying, and thrashing my arms and legs. Grandfather is aghast at the damage such a small person can manage in a short time. *Get up*, he roars. *Get up and go to the house. You're no good. You're no good for anything. Get out. You're a quitter. You'll never amount to anything.* I leave, go to the house, and enjoy the company of my dolls. Jim and Barbara continue weeding.

~ ~ ~

There are two authorities in life. One is the Bible; the other is Grandfather's interpretation of the Bible. I earn a penny for every Bible verse I memorize. The story of the wedding at Cana puzzles me. I ask Mother, *If wine is terrible, why did Jesus turn the water into wine? Why didn't he turn the wine into water?* She answers with a look that says, *Never ask that question again.* It is my first experience with inconsistencies in biblical interpretation.

~ ~ ~

Grandfather has rounded up the three of us. We are going to learn how to plant potatoes. The rows of hills make straight lines into eternity. Grandfather leads our brigade. He digs the exactly correct hole in the hill. Barbara follows with a bucket of seed potatoes, dropping three chunks into each hole. *Mind you put the eyes up*: is the beginning instruction. I am next with a bucket of fertilizer. *Only one spoon, don't spill, that fertilizer is expensive*: is the next instruction. Jim has the worst job of all, one that requires a judgment call. He is to put the soil back into the hole to cover the potatoes. *Mind how you tamp that soil, stay off the hills or you'll tear them down. Be careful you don't tampsoil too much.* The instructions continue with each hill of potatoes.

~ ~ ~

The garden needs weeding. Grandfather harnesses one of the horses to a small hand plow. He throws a blanket over the horse and harness. He places me on the blanket. The horse, a gentle Clydesdale mare, understands plowing. Everything goes well until we come to the row that ends in the windbreak. *Drive her up into the trees, I told you the ground by the trees needs cultivating,* he insists. The branches of the trees poke me everywhere. I grab the horse's mane and lie down on her back. *I told you to drive her into the trees. Can't you do what you're told? You'll never amount to anything if you can't do what you're told,* Grandfather bellows. Grandmother appears. She lifts me off the horse, scratched and howling. Grandfather and the mare cultivate the rest of the garden without further assistance from me.

~ ~ ~

Grandfather works for the Shorthorn Association. His territory is from Winnipeg to Vancouver. He advises farmers and ranchers on how to improve their herds.

Home from one of his trips, Grandfather orders us to bring him his grip, a huge leather suitcase that holds everything he needs for his travels. It takes the three of us to drag this suitcase into the dining room. He opens it with great ceremony, bringing forth the much-anticipated gift --- a large bag of jellybeans. *Divide these equally*, he admonishes Jim. Since he is the eldest, the weighty responsibility of proper care and handling of this treasure trove falls on his shoulders. We retreat to the bedroom where Jim spreads the jellybeans out for us to gaze at in all their multicolored glory. *One for me:* Jim places one in his pile. *One for you:* he places one in my pile, *One for me* he places one in his pile. *And one for you*, as he places one in Barbara's pile. When the distribution is over, his pile is larger than Barbara's or mine. I know I have been bamboozled. I leave to share my jellybeans with my dolls. One day, I resolve, I will find out how Jim is cheating.

~ ~ ~

Grandfather seats Barbara, Jim, and me at the dining room table along with stacks of the Winnipeg Free Press. Under his stern tutelage, we twist each sheet of newspaper into a taper. The tapers we make will be used to light the kerosene lamps. The ever-burning kitchen stove will ignite the tapers, thus saving the cost of using sulfur matches. The work of making these money saving devices is tedious and demanding. Grandfather truly believes the gates of Heaven open only to those who work hard and waste nothing. He wants to make sure we will be able to spend eternity with him.

~ ~ ~

When Grandfather drives, we sit quietly in the back. *Don't hang your arm out of that window*, Grandfather orders. *A child stuck an arm out of a window and a passing car just took it right off!* We consider Grandfather's warning and decide the risk is too awesome for experimentation.

~ ~ ~

Grandmother never wears her diamond rings when she goes into Winnipeg to see a doctor. She says doctors charge higher fees if they think she has money. *Dr. Jamieson knows I have diamonds but that doesn't matter because he is a friend of the family,* she explains.

~ ~ ~

On Christmas eve, a fresh linen cloth covers the dining room table. Grandmother allows me to help place the crèche in the middle of the table. Mary, Joseph and the Christ Child glow in the light of Christmas candles. Grandfather reads the Christmas story from Saint Luke. We feast on a stew rich with oysters from Chesapeake Bay. We savor glove oranges from Japan, candied ginger from China. Santa Claus will arrive during the night. He stops at our house first because we live closest to the North Pole.

~ ~ ~

Grandmother commandeers the three of us one morning. We load the wheelbarrow up with all the rhubarb from the cellar. We muscle the loaded wheelbarrow into the barnyard. As we pour the rhubarb into the pig trough, we notice it is bubbly and has a strange smell. Grandmother calls the pigs. They consume the dumped fruit with relish and then to our amazement, they begin to squeal, push each other around, fall in the trough and run in circles. After we have dumped all the rhubarb into the trough, Grandmother explains the fermentation of fruit. She warns us of the evil of alcohol, using the pigs as an object lesson. Later, after we discuss the experience, we decide the pigs seemed to be having a pretty good time.

~ ~ ~

Mother takes me to the schoolhouse where Mr. Pedon, the itinerant preacher, baptizes me. Mrs. White, who lives on a farm a mile away from us, also presents her six children for baptism. Mr. White stays home. Mrs. White weeps throughout the service. The Whites are Irish Catholic. It is my first ecumenical experience.

~ ~ ~

17

Grandfather culls the spring calves in early summer. The bull calves put their heads down, lean against the pen and moan the day they are de-horned and changed into steers. But, in a day or two they return to the pasture to graze, chew their cud, and munch the extra grain ration that will make them fat for market.

~ ~ ~

Bill Stokes looks like a batch of bread that has been left to set too long. He calls on the phone. He wishes to speak to Grandfather. Mother tells Mr. Stokes that Grandfather is on one of his trips. Mr. Stokes hems and haws. Finally, urgency overcomes inhibitions. Mrs. Bruce, he stammers to my mother, I need to make arrangements for your father's gentleman cow.

Barbara gets the mumps. Her face swells into painful puffiness, and we call her Bill Stokes.

~ ~ ~

When Grandfather and Grandmother drive together in the car, Grandmother sits close to Grandfather. That way, she can see the speedometer. If the needle goes past a certain number Grandmother reaches up to pat Grandfather on his shoulder. He always slows down.

~ ~ ~

Mother tries explaining to me that there is no Easter Bunny. I am indignant. Of course there is an Easter Bunny, I tell her. I saw him on the lawn this morning. The disclosure of Santa's true identity has been easy for me to accept. I have never seen him. But the rabbit? He is there for all to see. If chickens can lay eggs, well, why not a rabbit. Everyone knows the rabbit in Alice in Wonderland has a watch and white gloves, just like Grandmother.

~ ~ ~

Grandmother says smoking is a sin. All the hired men smoke. Mother smokes. Both she and Grandmother pretend they don't.

The usual Sunday guests, Dr. Stobart and his wife among them, have all gone home. The table has been cleared, the crumbs swept off the fresh tablecloth, the dishes washed up.

Mother tucks me into bed, listens to my prayers. In a moment of confidentiality I tell her I am going to smoke when I grow up. Mother seems surprised and asks me why. *Because it makes you beautiful, like Mrs. Stobart*, I whisper.

Mrs. Stobart doesn't think anyone knows she smokes, either.

~ ~ ~

We are going to have little pigs, I announce. Mother says no and explains it isn't the right time of year. *If you saw what I saw by the barnyard haystack, you would know we are going to have little pigs*, I insist. Several weeks later, the sow produces an out-of- season litter.

Miss Boyd, another Sunday dinner guest, teaches grade eleven in the Roland School. Roland has a big statue of a soldier who died in The War. Miss Boyd drives the ten miles from Roland to the farm in her own car. Tall and slender, she wears her curly gray hair cut short. The meal is over and dusk settles in. I wander into the sitting room to discover Grandfather wrapped tightly around Miss Boyd. I slip out of the room before they notice me.

Barbara and I are old women when I share my memory with her. Barbara says no such thing ever happened and even if it did, they were only playing kissy face. Barbara, I say, what I saw was no kissy face.

~ ~ ~

Grandfather brings a prospective cattle buyer home. I have never known anyone to act or smell like this man. Grandmother insists that he drink some coffee. He puts too much cream into the cup and the cream and coffee spill, leaving a large stain on the linen tablecloth. Grandmother is upset. I can tell by the way she sits in her chair.

Grandfather shows the cattleman to his bedroom before my bedtime. Usually guests are kept up late into the evening in long and animated conversations. He and Grandfather leave early the next morning, right after breakfast.

Storm windows have three holes at the bottom with a slat that can be moved to open one or all of the holes, allowing fresh air into the room. When we go outside to play we discover a large, yellow icicle hanging from the sill of the storm window belonging to the bedroom where the cattleman spent the night. We rush to tell Mother of our hilarious discovery. The cattleman, disoriented and unable to find the chamber pot, has urinated out of one of the conveniently spaced storm window holes.

Grandmother reminds us that humans and pigs suffer the same disgraceful behavior when drunk.

~ ~ ~

Grandfather and Mother, seated at the dining room table amid piles of stationery, envelopes, copies of *Shorthorn World*, and the typewriter, are having a discussion. Mother wants to go to work in Winnipeg. Grandfather says she has all the work she needs right where she is. The discussion continues until Grandmother comes into the dining room, takes Grandfather's arm, leads him into the bedroom, and shuts the door.

~ ~ ~

Mother, Jim, Barbara and I move to Saint Vital, a little town on the outskirts of Winnipeg. We share a house with Mother's widowed best friend, Aunt Lena, and her two daughters. The restrictions of city life are troublesome. Because the yard is small we run up and down all the stairs, from basement to attic. Outside games are hard on the interior of a house. My left arm goes through an upstairs bedroom window. Blood is everywhere.

An old lady and her little dog pay a visit. The dog pees on the chesterfield. When the old lady walks her dog past the house we children greet her with, Hello, Mrs. Pig, hello Mrs. Cow, hello, Mrs. Horse. She tells on us. We stop.

Mother gives Barbara and Jim twenty-five cents to take me to the barber for a haircut. There are two barbers to choose from. One is sober; one is always drunk but gives free suckers. They choose the one who dispenses suckers. He insists I am a boy and cuts my hair accordingly. When we get home, Mother cries. Before long, we move back to the farm.

~ ~ ~

In preparation for the celebration of Grandmother's and Grandfather's fortieth wedding anniversary, Grandmother has made it known that she expects a set of fine china for the occasion. The day arrives. The guests assemble. When Grandmother accepts the presentation of boxes of dishes, she opens just one box and removes just one plate of the ugliest crockery imaginable. Grandmother thanks Grandfather graciously. The evening is a success. The boxes remain unopened. The guests leave. Grandmother returns the one plate to the only box she opened.

A few days later, Grandfather leaves on another trip. The day after his departure, Grandmother takes the dishes out of all the boxes, sets the table with her anniversary dishes. Thereafter, these dishes are used for everyday meals.

~ ~ ~

I awaken early on my sixth birthday, knowing I will have been transformed, like Cinderella, during the night. I will be more beautiful than Snow White, smarter than the miller's daughter who spun flax into gold and with hair like Rapunzel. Snow White's image is not what I see reflected in Mother's mirror. It is my first experience with unrealistic expectations.

~ ~ ~

Grandfather says high-heeled shoes were invented by a woman who was kissed on the forehead.

~ ~ ~

Before we walk on the railroad tracks, Jim puts his ear on one of the rails. He hears the vibrations of the train long before we can see it, he says. Our safety assured we balance our way to Kane. Jim and Barbara move quickly along the rail. I spend most of my time jumping from tie to tie just to keep up.

~ ~ ~

Jim knows how to tell time by checking the sun's position in the sky. He knows where the prairie chicken hides her nest. After I promise to be really quiet, we hide in the tall grass and wait for her to bring her tiny brood safely home. He knows why the killdeer runs in circles pretending she has a broken wing. He knows the meadowlark builds her nest along the grasses close to the ditches where the plows cannot reach. He does not know why she sings all the time.

Jim shows us how to dam the snowmelt in the spring, making rivulets and waterfalls as the water flows into the dugout. He builds a Ferris wheel with his erector set, makes it go around by hooking it up to his toy steam engine which runs on alcohol. Jim knows everything.

~ ~ ~

Oatmeal is required eating every morning for breakfast. There is no negotiation on this requirement. We know that if we don't eat our porridge we will end up poor, or slothful, or a disgrace. Sometimes when no one is looking, Mother will put a little brown sugar on top of the bowl of oatmeal to make the required eating more palatable. The essential nutrition is served with good rich milk from the darling cows that provide us with an abundance of milk and cream and butter. Lady Eliza, the only cow ever to be called by name, receives extra loving care. We hand feed her to reward her for being old, and a good and faithful servant.

~ ~ ~

Grandmother gives me a piece of paper to use any way I wish. Seated at the dining room table I write:

Marion Gertrude Bruce
Kane
Manitoba
Canada

North American Continent
Western Hemisphere
Earth
The Universe

I finish writing. Grandmother picks up my piece of paper, reads it, folds it, and carefully puts it in her apron pocket.

~~~

Mr. Fredrickson lives across the road from our farm. He is from Germany and speaks English with a pronounced accent. He calls the three of us his little buggers. Mother explains that Mr. Fredrickson uses the term affectionately. In Canada, *bugger* usually means *fucker*.

Every fall Mr. Fredrickson helps slaughter the chickens. It is his specialty. He has a little knife with an extremely sharp blade. All the knives used for slaughter on Grandfather's farm are biblically sharp. Mr. Fredrickson shows up when we slaughter a hog. He makes the best sausage in the entire world.

~~~

Our radio is battery powered. When left to make our own choices, we tune into Radio Canada, the French-speaking station, even though we speak the King's English.

Because the radio has short wave capabilities, Mr. Fredrickson comes over one evening. He and Grandfather listen to a speech by Hitler being broadcast from Berlin. Mr. Fredrickson translates, struggling through the tears streaming down his face. At the end of the broadcast he says, *By Gott, Jim, der's gonna be anutter var.*

Barbara and Jim arrive home from school and we gather around the radio to listen to Little Orphan Annie, Jack Armstrong, the All American Boy and Dick Tracy. Mother, warned of the new technology and its possible dire effects on our minds, carefully censors our radio time. Jim and Barbara send each other coded messages on their Dick Tracy Decoder Ring. We drink Ovaltine on the advice of Little Orphan Annie. Later in the afternoon, we play school using the chalkboard and chalk. Jim and Barbara teach me the alphabet, numbers, how to write my name.

~ ~ ~

We live in the flyway of the Canada geese. Spring and fall are heralded by their noisy arrival. Grandfather never allows them to be hunted. *We have no need for meat*, Grandfather says.

Jim has permission to use the 22 rifle to shoot rabbits. They damage the trees in the windbreak. He sells the rabbits to the local mink farm for mink food. Some of the money he makes helps him buy more ammunition to shoot more rabbits.

~ ~ ~

Keeping the barn clean is a hard job. Every day the hired men clean and wash down the gutters. Once a week they muck out the stalls, wash them, and fill them with fresh straw. The manure pile grows with each passing week. In winter, it sends tendrils of steam into the air. Every spring the men load the rich mulch onto a piece of machinery called the manure spreader. The bed of this large horse-drawn wagon is a conveyor belt that moves the mulch into a spiked iron cylinder. The cylinder rotates, throwing the mulch evenly onto the ground. Sometimes I get to ride alongside one of the hired men who drives this fearsome machine. We sit on a seat, high above the contents of the load. Sometimes I get to hold the reins and say *gee* and *haw*. After the manure pile is distributed, the men plow and seed the ground. Grandfather's land produces bumper crops of oats, barley, wheat, flax and hay year after year. *The animals pay for their keep many ways*, Grandfather says.

~ ~ ~

Grandfather takes us driving on a Sunday afternoon to see how other people's crops are doing. Some of the fields are yellow with mustard blossom which means they won't get paid as much for their grain. Grandfather asks if we see that man out working in his field. *He'll never prosper working on the Sabbath*, Grandfather admonishes. Grandfather has never had a crop failure.

~ ~ ~

Mother has taken me into Winnipeg for a visit to the dentist. While Dr. Graham interviews Mother, I study Dr. Graham. He is tall and slender. His dark hair is turning gray. He wears a white suit and speaks softly. He escorts Mother and me into a white, strange smelling room. Dr. Graham lifts me into the big black chair. He tells Mother to leave. I eye him with suspicion.

He stands close to me and says, *Marion, I want you to open your mouth.*

I want my mother, I reply.

Open your mouth, he says in his soft voice.

Perhaps he is deaf, like Grandmother. I speak louder. *I want my mother.*

The doctor steps closer. *You can't have her,* he whispers.

I want my mother I inform him.

Open your mouth, he hisses.

No! I firmly respond.

He steps back and slaps me across the face. He is not prepared for the ferocity of my screams. Mother rushes in, removes me from the chair. We leave.

~ ~ ~

Sandy, the only cat ever allowed in the house, and I enjoy an unusual friendship. He seeks me out to curl around me. I grab his tail; swish him back and forth across the smooth linoleum on the kitchen floor. He extends his claws in a futile attempt to end his ride, yowling in full voice the whole time. Mother makes many attempts to stop our rough play. Nothing works. The cat returns again and again to cooperate in our unique sense of fun.

In the kitchen, Mother, Tina and Grandmother convert chokecherries into jelly. Seated on the floor, under the work counter, I watch their feet. Sandy wanders in the house and joins me.

A chokecherry, exactly the right size and shape to stuff up the cat's bum, roll off the counter onto the floor. The cat lets out an ear splitting screech and leaves. Mother reaches down and hauls me out from under the counter, administering corporal punishment even before Barbara, the eyewitness, can tell on me.

~~~

Grandmother sits at the dining room table while Mother writes down grain futures from the grain exchange's noon radio broadcast. After the broadcast, she transcribes the figures for Grandmother. Grandmother in turn works some algebraic equations on paper. Grandmother completes her calculations. Mother calls Mr. Loftus in Winnipeg. Mr. Loftus, Grandmother's attorney, buys and sells grain futures for her. Mother says Grandmother makes a tidy sum.

Grandfather rarely invests in the grain futures. Mother says when he does, he loses his shirt.

~~~

Grandmother always keeps a roll of bills in one of her shoes in the farthest back part of her closet. When Mother's only sister, Auntie Edna, comes home for a visit, she reprimands Grandmother for this unsafe habit. Grandmother's response is that she never has to make a trip to the bank and she is the only one who knows she has the money.

The long twilight of the Manitoba prairie is drawing to a close. Mother is getting frantic. Grandmother left early in the morning with the hired men who were taking a truckload of cattle into the city. The two men returned hours ago and they are as apprehensive as Mother as to Grandmother's whereabouts. A strange car heads down the lane, moving at a Snail's pace, headlights blazing. The vehicle stops at the house gate. Grandmother emerges. *I'm tired of being left on this farm without decent transportation*, is her only comment.

~ ~ ~

Jim torments me. He grabs my wrists, pins me on the floor, threatens to drool on my face. I scream, plead, try to kick him. Nothing works. Suddenly my mind floods with every word I was never supposed to hear. The obscenities flow from my mouth. Jim is so surprised by the extravagance of my language that he lets me go. It is my first experience with the power of the spoken word.

~ ~ ~

The implement shed, a long narrow building, houses the farm machinery. A large workbench with all the necessary tools fills the windowed end of the building. We are never allowed in this place. Too dangerous! we are told. We surreptitiously gain entrance, there to spend an afternoon happily pounding a wondrous assortment of nails into the hard dirt floor. Neither the building, the workbench, nor tools turn out to be injurious.

~ ~ ~

Grandfather, along with about twenty-five other cattlemen, is invited to go to Alberta to meet Edward, Prince of Wales. When Grandfather returns we wait the recounting of his experience. *What was he like?* we demand. *Dead drunk,* is Grandfather's reply. No further discussion takes place even when the commemorative picture of the event arrives.

~ ~ ~

Saturday morning, rich with our own carefully pocketed penny, we begin the mile trek to Kane. The distance provides us with sufficient time to debate the merits of the available candy from which we will make our weekly selection.

The little store across the road from the train depot has a large assortment of penny candy along with lamp wicks, soft drinks, matches, boot polish, tobacco in tins, cigarette papers, ready-made cigarettes for the ladies, coal oil, white gasoline, lamp chimneys, shoelaces, and sewing thread, but most important a patient owner who lets us browse at the candy display. I usually choose a jawbreaker because it will last most of the day.

En route, Mr. Penner hobbling towards Kane, waylays us. Mr. Penner is old and his feet hurt. He speaks in an accent different from Mr. Fredrickson's because Mr. Penner is a Mennonite and Mr. Fredrickson is a German. He engages us in a conversation in which he admonishes us as to the importance of good health. Mr. Penner points to his ragged tennis shoes and proudly announces, *I pay particular attention to my feet.* We hurry on to make our anticipated purchase, leaving old Mr. Penner lagging far behind where he cannot hear our derisive laughter.

~~~

Edward, uncrowned King of England, wants to marry Wallace Warfield Simpson, a twice-divorced American. *What can you expect from a drunkard?* Grandfather asks.

We chant, *Hark the Harold Angles sing, Wallace Simpson stole our king.* We chant, *I see London, I see France, I see Wally's underpants.* No one tells us to stop.

~~~

A long time ago, Grandfather had two big holes scooped out of the earth. The dugouts, filled with rainwater and snowmelt, provide water for all the animals. In the summer, dragonflies and crayfish abound. In the spring and fall, the Canada geese stop and rest during their noisy trips north and south. Only in the winter, when the dugouts turn to ice, are we allowed near their treacherous depths. Jim, in hockey skates, brooms the snow from the bumpy surface. Barbara glides on the freshly exposed ice. I follow, pushing an old kitchen chair ahead of me until I can learn to skate on my own.

~~~

Miss Anderson, my grade one teacher, also teaches grades two through grade five in the same room at Kane Consolidated School. She is a pretty blonde woman. I adore her. She becomes engaged to be married. Her fiancé gives her an expensive diamond ring. In early summer of 1936 she dies suddenly before she can be married. Her mother's extravagant insistence that Miss Anderson's engagement ring be buried with her shocks the community. It is a decision based on Mrs. Anderson's need to punish Miss Anderson's fiancé. Miss Anderson has died as the result of a botched abortion.

~~~

Mr. Siemens teaches grades six through eleven. Tall, sparse, physically fit, he controls his class through terror, dragging boys by the scruff of the neck over the tops of the desks, yanking girls' hair for minor infractions of his rules. To get promoted from one grade to the next requires a passing mark in departmental examinations. Mr. Siemens' no nonsense approach enables most students to pass the required yearly exam.

~~~

Jim comes home bloodied from schoolyard fights. Taunted by remarks from the bigger boys that Mother gets between the sheets with John Gunn, he defends her honor as best he can.

~~~

I am the only child in grade one who speaks English. Before too long, I can understand the German the other children speak. I would no more practice my newly acquired language at home than I would try to mimic the French words I hear on the radio. It is of no importance. By year's end, everyone in grade one speaks English.

~~~

I arrive home from school cranky and sullen. What a face, Mother teases. Tears roll down my cheeks. *Someone ate my lunch again today,* I whisper to her. Despite the closeness of the supper hour, Mother takes me to the kitchen, feeds me bread, butter, jam, and a glass of milk. *Whoever took your lunch is really hungry. They just wanted to eat something else besides a lard sandwich,* she explains. *Why don't they eat Barbara's lunch instead of mine?* I wonder. Mother pats my bottom, sends me on my way to play until she can call me to supper. When

Grandmother hears my tearful tale she hugs me, reminds me the Lord loveth a cheerful giver.

~ ~ ~

Every Friday afternoon, Miss Anderson expects all pupils from Kane Consolidated Schools to stand before the class to present a selected reading or a poem they have memorized. Reciting a short poem is a favorite choice. Rosalie, a member of grade five, defies authority one Friday with her recitation of, *Beans, beans are musical fruit, the more you eat the more you toot, the more you toot the better you feel, so I have beans for every meal.* A shocked silence follows. Her disgrace is such that I remember forever the verse after Rosalie's only recital.

~ ~ ~

Getting to school in the winter requires the services of a horse drawn van, heated by warmed stones placed on the floor. The driver stops the van at our door, in the dark, at seven thirty in the morning and deposits us back home, in the dark, at four thirty in the afternoon. I hate being crowded into that vehicle with all the other children. Most people don't waste much time or energy bathing in the winter and the smell of wet wool and unwashed bodies is unpleasant.

~ ~ ~

A tall man, accompanied by a large German shepherd, appears at the kitchen door. Mother greets the man warmly. *Hello, Bill. Who's your friend?*

Bill explains that the dog has failed at the police academy. He has driven the animal all the way from Winnipeg in hopes that Mother will be the rescuer. She reluctantly accepts her new role.

It turns out to be a happy decision.

Rex, the German Shepard and Fly, the Shetland pony and Jim round up the cattle from the pasture, walking them the long distance to the barn. They bring the horses into the barnyard at a dead gallop, manes and tails flying. Rex nips at their heels. Fly enjoys the challenge of keeping up with the Clydesdales. Everyone looks forward to this game every evening.

We take Rex gopher hunting. We wait quietly for a gopher to pop up from its hole. Rex grabs the pest and with one quick shake, places its lifeless body at our feet.

When the grass is tall he plays hide and seek with us. He hunts and hunts for us even though we know he can smell exactly where we are.

When the snow is too fresh to bear Fly's weight, Jim puts on his skis and harnesses Rex. They glide on top of the drifts to the depot, return with the mail and a copy of the Winnipeg Free Press.

Rex becomes violently ill. Doctor Stobart makes a professional call. Rex recovers.

Nights belong to the dog. Some mornings he is almost too tired to help Jim with chores.

Rex fears the prairie thunderstorms. When one comes up, he cowers under Mother's bed. Once he gets enmeshed in Mother's silk stockings. *If he weren't so frightened, I'd hit him*, Mother says, mourning her ruined hosiery.

~~~

I have decided it is the dog's birthday. Grandmother has taught me how to make cake. I spend the morning baking, using the toy utensils Grandmother has provided for toy cooking. During dinner I slip away from the table. Because no birthday candles are available, I decorate the cake with toothbrushes. I walk the decorated cake around the table while singing Happy Birthday to Rex. There is laughter. I cry. Grandfather swoops down and grabs me by one arm. He whisks me into the bedroom. He is going to give me a whipping for crying. I howl in outrage, my hurt feelings turning into fury. I try to climb up his arm to reach his face. I know if I can reach his face I can kill him. The battle is short lived. Grandfather, drops me on the bed and leaves.

~~~

In winter, we are not allowed outdoors at night. Except on this special night; we are bundled, enfolded, wrapped in wool, to venture out into the darkness. *Look, Boodie, the northern lights!* Jim excitedly points me in the correct direction. This is the same Jim who told me to stick my tongue on the clothesline pole if I wanted to see China. I decide the flickering pastel lights look like trails left by fairy wings or a melting rainbow. Before Mother can whisk us back into the house, Jim shows me how to stamp and twist my booted feet in the snow to make it crack, whip like, in the heavy air. Once inside the house, we shed our woolen cocoons. Later, after we are tucked into multi-blanketed beds, Grandmother reads us another chapter of Peter Pan.

~~~

Mother calls me to look out the window with her. Nothing moves in the dark subzero air. See how the moon has blanketed the snow with diamonds, she says.

~~~

The King George and Queen Elizabeth of England visit Canada. When they arrive in Winnipeg, Mother takes us into the city to view their Majesties and the parade given in their honor. The city swept fresh and clean, is swathed in Union Jacks. At the appointed hour we stand curbside, taffeta bows stiffly at attention, Jim elegant in his new corduroy breeches.

The Mounties, red coated for this most dressed of dress parades, prance past us on their matched sorrels.

The king and queen drive slowly past us in an open touring car. She, in powder blue, acknowledges the crowd's adulation by graciously waving her wee, gloved hand.

To properly close the parade properly, the Queen's Own Cameron regiment comes swirling down the street, led by the regimental pipes and drums. I am swept along with them, carried away by their skirling pipes, their cadenced drums. Mother runs down the street to return me to my proper place on the sidewalk. Tearfully I watch the regiment disappear out of my life.

~ ~ ~

Everybody lives a mile away from our farm. George and Nerta Miller live a mile to the east. They have no children because Nerta doesn't like children. I can tell she especially doesn't like me from the way she speaks at me. *Nice little girls don't use too much of their pretty crayons on just one picture,* she says when viewing my coloring book. George loves children. He is extravagant, Nerta says. He buys bananas and gives them to me, to share with Jim and Barbara. Grandfather says George is extravagant because when his horses get old, he puts them out to pasture. *They worked hard; they deserve a rest,* George reasons. Nerta reminds him of his extravagance so much that he has an affair with their hired girl.

~ ~ ~

The White family lives a mile to the west of our farm. There are six children, three boys and three girls. Mr. White doesn't own the farm. Uncle Jim Miller does. Maybe that is why Mr. White doesn't work very hard on the land. I see him just once, leaning on his shovel, studying the ground. Mrs. White never asks us to come inside for anything to eat or drink.

We take Fly, Jim's Shetland pony, when we go to the White's house. The Cowie family lives on a farm a mile south of the White's. They raise Shetlands. The Cowie house doesn't have any paint on the outside. They probably don't farm much because there is no Mr. Cowie. When Martha Cowie knows we are going to be playing at the Whites, she rides over on one of her ponies. Then she and Jim race to the end of the White's lane. Or sometimes they just see who can get their pony to buck the longest.

~ ~ ~

Mr. Fredrickson lives on the farm a mile to the south of us. He lives with his invalid wife, and his daughter, son-in-law and grandchildren, Gladys and Donny. When we go to the Fredrickson's house to play, we always play cops and robbers. The Fredricksons don't think it is too rowdy for us to pretend to be John Dillinger and the FBI.

~ ~ ~

Jim, Barbara and I have been invited to Nerta Miller's for tea. Barbara, and I, resplendent in Stuart plaid skirts, and Jim, elegant in his hated corduroy breeches that make whistling sounds when he moves, walk the mile from our house to the Miller's. No cutting through fields, no sharing the pony on this journey. Our family's reputation is at stake. We are expected to behave like children of landed gentry. Grandfather signs his letters Jas. B. Davidson, Esquire.

We arrive footsore and thirsty from trudging the mile of gravel road, anxious from the struggle of trying to stay clean. Nerta ushers us into the sun porch where she has set out a wondrous tea. Linen covers the tea table. She has arranged the tea sandwiches and cakes on fine china. The teapot reposes in its cozy. I find the nearest chair. Seating myself before being invited to take my ease, I ask, *When do we eat?*

It is the last time Nerta attempts to civilize us.

~ ~ ~

Only one story is told about Grandmother. Grandfather had to leave to go to Winnipeg. He rode Grandmother's saddle horse, Lady, the fifty miles because it was faster than walking. While he was gone, the prairie caught fire. Grandmother took her two little girls, my auntie and mother, out to sit on the steps of their small wooden house. There they watched the fire get closer and closer. *Then the wind changed,* Grandmother said.

~ ~ ~

A sultry summer day in southern Manitoba, Grandmother stops the car at a gas station. Inside the station, a tantalizing cooler full of soft drinks turns us into shameless beggars. Hot and thirsty, we promise to be good. We coax, we implore, until Grandmother succumbs. *Cokes!* we shout at her. She frowns, walks into the station and returns with one, open, bottle of Coke. We are disheartened but not surprised. *Look,* she says as she pours the icy drink onto the dusty grass. We watch, horrified, as the precious liquid drain into the vegetation. *If Coca Cola turns the good grass brown,* she says, *think what it will do to your stomach.* We settle for Orange Crush, crème soda.

~~~

Something bad has happened in one of the fields with one of the horses. Grandfather, draped over John Gunn, has to be helped into the house. White faced and sweaty, Grandfather holds his right arm close to his chest, sits down heavily on a dining room chair. Mother rings up the operator who rings up Dr. Jamieson on the telephone. Dr. Jamieson agrees with Mother. Grandfather should be driven to his office in Carman right away.

The situation must be serious because Grandfather does not attempt to change out of his work clothes while Mother brings the car around to the dining room door. John Gunn fixes a glass of milk with sugar, an egg, a large measure of brandy for Grandfather to drink. He helps Grandfather into the back seat of the car, fixes the pillow and blanket that Grandmother has supplied. Mother drives off with Grandfather singing lustily from the backseat.

After Grandfather is safely on the twenty-five mile gravel road to Dr. Jamieson's office, Grandmother invites John Gunn to join her in a cup of coffee. Ted is a gentle, hardworking horse, and Grandmother wants John to explain the sudden viciousness of the animal.

John relates the series of events to her. Grandfather was driving the team. He didn't think Ted was pulling his share of the load. Grandfather hit Ted with the reins, yelled at him, got off the wagon, hit Ted on the neck, yelled at him, hit him on the face, and yelled at him. Ted balked, which made Grandfather so angry that he gathered a pile of straw under Ted's belly. It was only after Grandfather set fire to the straw that Ted kicked him.

Grandmother asks if Ted is hurt. John says no, but he is certainly glad that Ted didn't kill Mr. Davidson. Grandmother thanks John, sends him back to the fields to finish the work.

Later that evening Mother and Grandfather return from Carman, Grandfather with a bottle of codeine and his arm in a cast.

Together Grandmother and Mother get Grandfather into bed.

In reporting his condition to Grandmother, Mother says Grandfather has a simple fracture of the bones in his lower arm. He didn't seem to mind the ride to Carman as he sang all the way and kept singing while his arm was being X-rayed and cast. He slept on the way home because the doctor gave him something for pain before they left.

A week later Grandfather leaves on another trip. He can drive just fine because the cast does not impair the use of his fingers.

That night Grandmother begins reading us the story of Black Beauty. From this story we learn that being bad to a horse is a worse sin than drinking brandy with egg and milk.

~ ~ ~

When Grandfather sings "Little Annie Laurie Is My Sweetheart", he really means me.

~ ~ ~

Grandmother keeps a house that can respond to almost any illness. A glass of hot water with lemon juice before breakfast promotes good health. If lemons are scarce, a teaspoon of vinegar is substitued. A glass of warm water with a teaspoon of bicarbonate of soda wards off a cold. Should this prescription fail, honey and lemon juice soothe the cough. Homemade mustard plasters draw congestion from the chest, unless you are Barbara. The plaster takes the skin from her chest, which makes her cry worse than when she was sunburned. Gold Thread, carefully stored in a small airtight tin, banishes canker sores with its bitterness. Oil of cloves soothes a toothache. Tobacco smoke, blown gently into the offending ear, eases the pain. A hot flax poultice applied to a boil localizes the infection, promotes healing. The best cure comes from the moldy bread Grandmother keeps stored in a damp, warm place. An infected wound is immediately treated with moldy bread, first soaked in warm milk, held firmly in place with a bandage made from worn-out linen sheets. The poultice, changed often, heals the wound quickly. *No need for blood poisoning,* Grandmother says.

~ ~ ~

Some of the steers have warbles, which makes Grandfather unhappy. The price of steer hide diminishes when warbles, left untreated, scar the hide. John Gunn shows the hired men how to locate the telltale knot, lance the hide with a small, sharp knife, pop the offending larva out, stomp it in the concrete gutter, repeat the process until all the larvae have been removed. The steers don't seem to mind the procedure.

I pay you men good wages to keep this barn clean, Grandfather explains to the men. *You get good grub, all you can eat, and a warm, dry bed. The least you can do is see things are kept clean enough so we don't have flies. Confound It!* he says.

When Grandfather says, *Confound It,* the whole world better watch out.

~ ~ ~

Twice a day the men bring the milk into the basement to be separated. The milk separator, a huge stainless steel machine, has special disks that allow cream to be separated from whole milk by Jim turning its heavy handle. After each use, Grandmother takes the separator apart, scrubs and scalds the many parts until everything shines like new.

In the spring when the cows are let out into fresh pasture, they produce onion-flavored milk. The men don't bother to bring the milk to the house then. They feed it to the pigs, who don't seem to notice the taste.

Grandmother stores the separated cream in big covered crocks in the basement where it stays cool and fresh until there is enough to churn. Jim helps pour the cream into the churn. The churn looks like an old oak barrel that sits in a wrought iron cradle. Jim and Grandmother take turns pushing its metal handle back and forth, changing the cream into butter and buttermilk.

Grandmother sells the extra butter to the Fitzhenrys who own the general store in Myrtle. She says her butter is the best because she works out all the moisture. She sells the extra eggs to the Fitzhenrys too.

~ ~ ~

The lady who teaches Barbara to play the piano for twenty-five cents a lesson lives in Myrtle. I don't like piano lessons. The lady cannot coax me to sit up to the piano or name the notes in my music book. She can't take money for my lesson with a clear conscience she tells Mother. It is my first failed attempt at musicianship.

~ ~ ~

I am always introduced to strangers as Jim Davidson's granddaughter.

~ ~ ~

When Grandmother expects important mail, she drives to Kane to meet the train. If she takes us with her, she makes sure we stand far back on the platform as the train pulls into the station. The force of a moving train can suck you right in under the wheels, she warns.

I love the grumbling of the ground as the train pulls alongside the platform, steam swooshing in enormous billows, the bell clanging an unnecessary warning.

Sometimes Grandmother gives each of us a penny to put on the track. We wait impatiently for the train to pull out, admire our flattened penny, and show it later to envious friends.

~ ~ ~

Grandmother and Grandfather own a cottage at Victoria Beach. We leave for the beach after Dominion Day when the ice is off Lake Winnipeg. The only way we can get there is by train. At the depot Grandmother's big trunk, packed with everything we need for the summer, is loaded on the baggage car. We climb aboard the passenger car with Grandmother.

The Indians who live around the lake all year stop by the cottage with their morning's catch of catfish. Grandmother pays twenty-five cents for six fillets which she says is a little dear but worth the money. Later in the morning, Indian children come by to sell us freshly picked blueberries. Grandmother bakes scones to serve with the berries. She bakes oatmeal cookies in the little cast iron stove in the kitchen. We share our treats with the squirrels and chipmunks. By the end of summer, the squirrels and chipmunks wait for us at the back door.

We go down to the water dressed in bathing suits, hats, little rubber wading slippers. Grandmother slathers us with her version of sun tan lotion made by mixing equal parts of vinegar and olive oil.

Jim and Barbara are allowed to swim out to the Rock.

Barbara gets sun burned.

We lose our wading slippers the first day.

After supper, we break a twig from a tree branch and use it to keep the clouds of mosquitoes away because the citronella Grandmother makes us rub on our skin has no effect. We walk down to the train depot where the store is like the one at Kane, except this store sells ice cream as well as penny candy. The five-cent, vanilla only, ice cream cone lasts all the way back to the cottage.

Grandfather arrives unexpectedly to make sure the cottage is sound. Grandmother and Grandfather have a discussion about the soundness of the roof. While we are eating the noon meal, Grandfather goes outside and climbs a ladder up to the roof. We can hear him walking around. We hear a thump, a clatter, a thud, a silence. Grandmother continues eating. *I told him not to go up there, she says.*

At Victoria Beach, the trees grow right down to the water.

The air smells like Christmas.

Lady Slippers bloom along the pathway to the outhouse.

The pitch from the trees is almost as good to chew as a stick of Wrigley's gum.

Sunlight, sifted through the trees, makes lacy shadows.

During a storm we don't go down to the water because it is too dangerous.

We sleep warm in our feather beds.

No one is ever cross or in a hurry.

We read books anytime we want.

We don't worry about manners at mealtime.

Grandmother shows us how to make a toy canoe from birch bark.

In a moment of wild abandon, Grandmother recites: *I know a shoemaker who lives in Jamaica who wiped himself on a piece of brown paper, the paper was so thin that his finger went in and oh what a mess that shoemaker was in.*

She clasps her tiny hands over her burning face and pleads, *Children, children, never tell your mother, promise me.*

We promise. We never tell Mother. We never forget the verse.

~ ~ ~

The only way out of Victoria Beach is by train, which leaves for Winnipeg in the late afternoon. One morning I don't feel well. Grandmother packs up everything, we board the train. Mother meets us at the depot in Winnipeg. She drives the fifty miles to Carman as fast as she can, slowing down when I lean out the window to throw up. We meet Dr. Jamieson at his office.

When Dr. Jamieson comes to the farm for a visit, I hide under the bed. I hate him.

He examines me on his old leather couch, hurries us over to the hospital where I was born. He performs an emergency appendectomy. Three days later, Mother drives me home, slowly, over the twenty-five miles of gravel road.

Arriving home, Mother puts me in her bed. She tells me not to move. Mother gives me a bell to ring if I need anything. The bell makes the nicest tinkling sound. I ring it often.

It is summer, and I have a lot to do, Mother explains, as she removes the bell from the bedside table.

I am hot, the bandage is uncomfortable. I work the adhesive tape away from the itchy spots on the right side of my stomach and back, then on the left side. I decide to look out the window. I slide out of bed. The massive bandage hits the floor about the same time my feet do. I examine my belly in amazement. I find Mother, Tina and Grandmother at work in the kitchen. I demand to know why all those black things are sticking out of my tummy. Work stops. Mother takes my hand, leads me back to the bedroom, explaining about the belly wound, the catgut stitches. *The stitches are to hold you together until you can grow back together again,* she says. *You must be very careful,* she says. *You must walk slowly and not run or jump,* she says, and puts me back to bed.

After supper, everyone is busy again. I slip out of bed, head for the barn, climb over the eight-foot barnyard gate, get a bucket of oats for Fly, see the evening star, make a wish, stumble into the pig wallow. The pigs are as surprised as I am. I scramble from this hole of pigs and stinking muck, climb back over the barbwire-laced eight-foot barnyard fence, utter piercing screams as I race back to the house. Grandmother comes outside to investigate. She calls to Barbara, keeping me on the concrete apron of the steps leading to the kitchen porch. Barbara brings pitcher after pitcher of water to wash away the stench, the slime, the mud. Grandmother deftly cleans the wound and its exposed stitches.

Your sister is going to die, she announces to Barbara.

Two weeks later, Mother takes me back to Carman to have Dr. Jamieson remove the stitches. I ask Mother to stay in the car while I go into the hospital by myself. I do not mention the pig wallow incident to my new friend, Dr. Jamieson.

~ ~ ~

Grandma Bruce lives far away, in Carman.

Once in a while Mother takes us to visit this mysterious lady because she is my father's mother.

Grandpa Bruce is dead. He has been dead for a long time.

Aunt Ag has been dead longer than Grandpa Bruce.

Grandma Bruce lives with Aunt Mary and Uncle Leish in the house Grandma and Grandpa Bruce built after they came to Canada and got married.

Aunt Mary teaches school in Carman.

Auntie Anne lives in Calgary.

Auntie Helen is a nurse. She lives in Brandon.

Mother says none of the Bruce women are decent housekeepers.

Uncle Bob teaches school in Calgary.

Uncle Tommy has TB and lives in the sanitarium at Ninette.

Mother says Uncle Tommy got sick from working at the curling rink without warm clothes or enough food when he was a growing boy.

I think Uncle Leish did something bad. I ask Mother if he robbed a bank. Mother says, *Certainly not, and where on earth did you ever get such an idea?*

Grandma Bruce sounds just like John Gunn when she talks. She calls Barbara and me her little kettles.

Grandma Bruce is tall and bony. She has sad eyes.

～～～

None of the hired men let me help them at milking time.

Ladies don't milk cows, Grandmother says.

John Gunn finally relents and makes room for me at the milking stool. No matter how hard I try, I cannot get any milk from the cow's teat. John makes me move out of the way when the cow gives warning twitches with her tail.

The barn cats line up in a row at milking time waiting for someone to shoot a stream of milk at them. They sit up on their hind legs and lick at the milk. It is the only time they are given anything to eat. Their job is to catch the fat mice who live in the barn.

~ ~ ~

We are never allowed to watch the slaughter of any animal. Once Barbara sneaks into the barn and peeks. She is not caught, saving everyone a lot of trouble!

Late one afternoon John Gunn takes us to a sheltered side of the barn. He tells us to stay there. He returns with a lamb in his arms. It only takes him a few minutes to change the lamb into meat for the table. We discuss our experience with no one, not even with each other.

~ ~ ~

Grandmother comes into the house from the barn. *Well, Leonora,* she says to our mother, *your children are going to die. I just found them drinking out of the horse trough.*

~ ~ ~

The week's supply of bread is made every Wednesday. To begin, Mother gets out the large blue enamel container with handles. She never measures any of the ingredients. *There is no need,* she says. She mixes water saved from the boiled potatoes with flour, yeast, butter, sugar and salt before we leave for school at 7:30 AM. Arriving home at 4:30 PM, we feast on the still-warm bread, which we slather with butter supplied by Lady Eliza and her sisters.

~ ~ ~

Grandmother has a rack for making toast. The rack, hinged in the middle, accommodates four slices of bread. Grandmother slices a loaf of bread so that each slice is exactly the same thickness, allowing the bread to toast evenly when she lays the neat slices in the rack on the hot stovetop. She flips the rack over at precisely the correct moment, turning the bread golden brown. When trying to reduce, Grandmother cuts her slices of bread extra thin. Her toast lasts longer when she eats the crisp little slices without butter or jam.

Because Grandmother never loses any weight, she has to wear a heavy corset summer and winter.

Grandmother has a glandular disturbance, Auntie Edna says.

~ ~ ~

The Watkins Man arrives every fall after the crops are harvested. He drives a special automobile with little compartments for every spice ever made. He sells real vanilla and artificial vanilla. He and Grandmother discuss the merits of each. *The artificial is cheaper, the real uses much less,* the Watkins Man confides to Grandmother. She agrees that real vanilla is the better buy. She buys lemon extract because sometimes it is not possible to get a fresh lemon.

When Grandmother uses the Watkins Man's spices she tells me what part of the world they came from. She says, *If it weren't for the British Empire our food wouldn't be so tasty.*

~ ~ ~

The Ladies' Aid Society is meeting at our house. I know, because Grandmother and Mother have put the quilting frame in the sparkling clean sitting room. The ladies arrive, put their hats and coats on the bed in Grandmother's bedroom, drink a cup of coffee, secure the quilt properly on the frame. They chatter and stitch the day away, stopping for the midday meal, then again for tea in the afternoon. I am not allowed to interfere with their activities or listen to their secrets. By late afternoon, the quilt completed, they leave for home to fix supper for their families.

~ ~ ~

Grandmother says that when she was growing up all her clothes were sewn by hand. She owns a Singer sewing machine. Working the foot pedal makes the needle go up and down. Grandmother allows no experimenting with this machine. *It's a precision instrument,* she explains. Either Mother or Grandmother makes all our clothes using the treasured Singer. But Jim's clothes are purchased from the T. Eaton Company, except for the corduroy breeches Auntie Edna sends him from the United States.

~ ~ ~

Times are hard; men without jobs knock on the kitchen door to ask for work and something to eat. After completing a simple task, Mother or Grandmother fixes a hearty meal on the back porch, then sends them on their way with a bundle of food.

Our hired men usually manage all the work but today an extra hand is needed in the field. The man who came looking for food is given a real job.

Barbara takes the mid-afternoon lunch out to the men and is waylaid by the new hire. Before she can hand him his food, he undoes his pants and shows her his penis. Barbara finishes delivering the rest of the lunches, returns to the house, reports her experience to Mother.

The new hire is not at the supper table.

~ ~ ~

We have two kinds of chickens, those who lay eggs and those who will be fried for supper.

The laying hens are confined to the hen house and its fenced yard.

The chickens who get to run around aren't good layers. Or else they are starting to look like roosters. The ones who start to look like roosters get to be our first fresh chicken supper of the year.

The hen house smells of whitewash, dusty straw, dusty feed, dusty oyster shells. Mother lets me help her gather eggs if I promise to be careful. *It took the hen all day to make that egg. It would be a shame to be careless with her hard work*, Mother says.

I watch a hen lay an egg. She makes a face, sighs several times, stands up, does a squawky dance, hops down off the nest. I think it would be nice to let her keep her egg. *The hen's job is to lay another egg tomorrow,* Mother says as she gathers the still-warm egg into her basket.

Sometimes a chicken forgets to lay her eggs in the nest. Sometimes we find them. They always smell bad when Jim breaks them open with a stick.

Jim says eggs are hen fruit.

~ ~ ~

On a windy day, the clouds make patterns on the ocean of green wheat.

~ ~ ~

One of the tools housed in the implement shed is a huge whetstone. Using its foot pedal, John Gunn spins the heavy wheel at a high speed to sharpen the butcher knives, kitchen knives, and scissors. When he sharpens the hoes and shovels, sparks fly.

The whetstone must be a precision instrument because we are not supposed to play with it either.

Grandfather, the only person to ever touch the carving knife, uses a long, pointy steel to keep it razor sharp. With great authority he sharpens this dangerous knife at table, just before he carves the turkey or a roast.

~ ~ ~

In the spring, after the lambs are born, John Gunn shears the sheep. He uses a special machine. The shears look just like the barber's, except the sheep shears are much bigger. The man working the foot pedal makes the clippers go fast or slow depending on John's instructions. After the sheep are shorn, they are run through sheep dip, which smells awful but kills the ticks.

Everything on the farm is from Scotland---horses, cattle, sheep, the pony. We are all from Scotland, too. John Gunn, the sheep and Fly have actually been there.

I don't think Grandfather likes the sheep because one day they just aren't there anymore.

~ ~ ~

We don't wear green on Saint Patrick's Day. We are not allowed to. We are not allowed to wear orange either.

~ ~ ~

When the weather changes from hot and humid to hot and dry, the hired men move some of the machinery out of the implement shed. They climb over, under, disappear into the threshing machine as they overhaul it. Its moving parts must work smoothly. They grease the innards of the binder and mower. They repack the wheels of the grain wagons with fresh axle grease. The axle grease only looks like taffy.

Jim helps by bringing the correct tools to the men. Sometimes he helps fix a part of a machine only his smaller hands can reach.

Grandfather purchases all the necessary supplies of grease, oil, gasoline and new binder twine. He makes sure last year's leftover twine is used first. Grandfather does not tolerate delays caused by inadequate supplies, repairs, or mistakes, once the race to harvest the grain begins.

A hired man drives the mower, pulled by a team of Clydesdales, into a field of ripe grain. Another hired man follows behind with the binder pulled by another team of Clydesdales. Grandfather and the rest of the hired men walk behind the binder, gather the sheaves, stook them into long, orderly rows.

John Gunn uses the John Deere tractor to haul the thresher into a field of stooked grain.

The threshing crew arrives the next morning.

Mother, Grandmother, and Tina rise to dress in the half-light of early morning. They fix a breakfast of bowls of steaming oatmeal, milk, pots of fresh, strong coffee, cream, sugar, and mounds of eggs, potatoes, bacon, piles of toast, butter, and jam. The dining room table empties and fills three times before all the men, including our own hired hands, leave for the fields.

The women spend the day preparing potatoes, vegetables from the garden, fried chicken, bread and pies and roasted slabs of beef. *Hungry men don't work well*, Grandfather says.

Barbara helps with dishes, goes with Grandmother to take the Mid-morning and mid-afternoon coffee and sandwiches out to the field, helps clear away the evening meal, and put the kitchen into working order for the next day's production of sturdy food.

At mealtime the men come in from the fields, hot and dusty from threshing. They wash their hands and faces in basins of water, lather up with cakes of soap, dry off on old towels provided for them on the back porch.

First light finds Jim at work with the men, milking cows, feeding and watering the horses and other livestock. The men hitch up the horses to the grain wagons. Before Jim and the hired men end their day, they milk cows, feed and bed down the horses, tend the other livestock.

Dust generated by the thresher makes Jim sick, especially the dust from the oats. His eyes and nose swell. He wears a big kerchief over his face, but it doesn't help him breathe more easily. He doesn't sleep at night. Mother puts cool, baking powder compresses on his arms, legs, chest to ease his itchy rash. Nothing stops his coughing.

During one of the grain harvests, Jim becomes seriously ill. Mother sends for Dr. Edwards. Dr. Edwards, a morphine addict, lives in Myrtle. He became addicted to morphine during the influenza epidemic following World War I. To keep going, he took morphine, sleeping in his buggy as he made rounds, mostly to sign death certificates. The epidemic abated. His addiction did not. The community, ever mindful of his sacrifice, allows him to continue practicing medicine. When he arrives to examine Jim, he is so unsteady on his feet that Grandmother follows around behind him with a chair. His stethoscope leaves a trail of red blotches on Jim's chest. *Pneumonia,* he finally pronounces. Muttering dire warnings about the future of Jim's health, the doctor lurches out to his car and drives away.

Once a team pulling a wagon full of grain ran away when Jim was driving. Probably Grandmother decided Jim was too young to manage such a hard job because he doesn't drive a grain wagon anymore.

My job is to stay out of the way.

The weather holds, the threshing completed. New haystacks gleam in the stubbled fields.

Our granaries burst with new grain to feed the livestock until the next harvest.

Roy Welch, the elevator operator at Kane, successfully oversees the weighing and storing of our excess grain. He brags of another accident-free harvest. Sometimes when delivering a wagon full of grain, a man will slip and fall into the elevator's huge grain bins and drown.

As the trucks carrying the threshing crew to the next farm begin to leave, one of the men doffs his hat at Mother. *You sure did feed us good, Missus*, he says.

~~~

After the grain is harvested, Mr. Fredrickson comes by to help slaughter the chickens. Mother, Grandmother, Tina, and I dress the chickens, making them ready for canning. So that I can reach the counter, John Gun has made a special little stool me.

Mother always names the chicken guts as I draw them from the still-warm chicken carcass. I never cut into the little gall bladder by the gizzard because its green bile would make the meat taste bad. I carefully keep the germ-laden intestines intact. The pink lungs make squishy noises when I poke them. The windpipe works just like an accordion. Grandmother shows me how to disjoint the carcass carefully. I never cut myself with the sharp knife.

After a hog is slaughtered, Grandmother cures hams, turns the side meat into bacon in a special spot in the basement.

Winter is coming.

~~~

When the blizzard hits, coal and three barrels of apples shipped in from back East fill the basement with a reassuring scent. The shelves in the cellar pantry are stacked in ordered rows with summer's canned surplus. Huge crocks of eggs preserved in silicate of soda rest along side huge crocks of new pickles in their brine. The earthy essence of the full potato bin completes the winter potpourri.

Mother has carefully tucked away the supply of raisins, walnuts, and olives so that we can't find them to share with the dog.

The men have stacked the kitchen porch with enough birch logs to keep the huge iron range fueled during the storm. Grandmother has seen to it that the cupboards are stocked with flour, sugar, tea, coffee, yeast, salt and spices.

The Aladdin Lamp, a technological leap in lighting, allows us to sit around the table at night with light bright enough to read, play Monopoly, knit, work a piece of embroidery, play cribbage or solve a jigsaw puzzle. Because no one but Mother or Grandmother is allowed to care for this lamp, I ask Grandmother to explain what makes it works. *By magic*, she says. *That's why it's called Aladdin.*

To ensure a safe journey from house to barn during the storm, John Gunn ties a pre-measured piece of rope to his waist. Dressed in heavy woolen long johns, woolen work pants, woolen shirt, woolen sweater, coveralls, woolen socks, work boots covered with galoshes, woolen hat, two woolen mufflers, work gloves covered with woolen mittens and a woolen Mackinaw, only then is he able to venture out and secure the other end of the rope to the gatepost by the kitchen porch. When he has traversed the length of the rope, he will know he is close to the barnyard gate. He finds the gate. He secures the rope to that gatepost. The other hired men follow the rope to the barn. This hazardous journey takes place twice a day to make sure the cows are comfortably milked. Fresh water, hay and food are served to all the residents. Doors and windows are made secure. They must not blow open. The cattle and horses, all registered Shorthorns and Clydesdales, make more money than the wheat Grandfather produces. Their care is paramount.

When the storm exhausts itself, travel is impossible. Our radio keeps us informed of world events even if the train cannot get to the depot with the Winnipeg Free Press.

Mother and Grandmother use their leisure time to knit woolen socks, sweaters, mufflers and our newest pair of angora mittens. When the angora mittens get wet, they aren't pretty anymore.

I learn the basics of addition and subtraction by playing cribbage. We put last year's jigsaw puzzles together faster than this year's new ones. A bottle of brandy reposes in a kitchen cupboard to ward off death should it threaten one of the animals or the hired help. With the furnace banked, we sleep soundly in our Hudson Bay blankets, at ease with the leisurely pace of winter living.

~ ~ ~

The rush of sledding down the snow bank caused by the snow drifting over the tops of the windbreak is nothing compared to the knowledge that when I climb to the top of the drift, I am standing on top of the trees.

~ ~ ~

I see an ermine scamper away from the barn. Excitedly I report my sighting to Grandfather. *It's really just a weasel in its winter coat,* he says. I wonder if King George of England knows the truth about ermine.

~ ~ ~

When I can't seem to recover from a winter cold and sore throat, Mother sends for Dr. Jamieson. He arrives by train because the twenty-five miles of winter roads from Carman to Kane are impassable by car. He diagnoses my high fever and painfully swollen leg joints as symptoms of rheumatic fever.

He returns to Carman, leaving a regimen of complete bed rest, a liquid diet and a large brown bottle of codeine tablets to control the pain.

At the beginning of the fever, Grandmother and Mother dab oil of wintergreen on my knees and ankles, wrap my legs in cotton wool to hold in the heat. At night Mother whips together cream, sugar and vanilla. She places the mixture on the kitchen porch. A few minutes later she feeds me the frozen confection.

To keep my bed from being touched, only Mother comes into my room, except when the linens need to be changed. Then the hired men come in, each to taking a corner of the bottom sheet. They raise me high enough for Mother and Grandmother to put fresh linens underneath me. Not even the comfort of an extra codeine tablet stops me from crying out with pain.

Eventually the fever subsides. I stop asking if it is time for a tablet from the brown bottle. I am allowed one pillow under my head, then two. I sit up in bed to read, color, take food from the bedside table. I am wrapped in sweaters, mufflers and blankets, taken to the dining room table and placed on it like a prized doll. The porch door is opened. I see the snow melting in the fields, and inhale the crisp prairie air. Schoolwork appears among my books. The weather warms into spring. I am out of bed and dressed. My legs have forgotten how to walk.

I recover, heart intact. For several years Mother feeds me a syrupy tonic of vitamins and excuses me from rigorous physical activities, regular school attendance, chores, and discipline. Tucked into bed at the first cough or sneeze, never to ice skate again, I wrap up my isolation in books.

~ ~ ~

Grandmother saves string. She winds every piece that comes into her possession onto a large ball, which she stores in a kitchen cupboard. She uses the string to teach us how to play cat's cradle, truss a roast, or a turkey.

Her favorite source of string comes from the carefully wrapped packages Eaton's sends us on the train. Before we can unwrap the package, we must untie the string. Cutting the knots would be easier—take less time. We offer to get the scissors. Instead, Grandmother recites:

If a string is in a knot,

Patience will untie it.

Patience will do many things.

Did you ever try it?

If 'twas sold in any store

You and I would buy it,

But you and I must get our own,

No others can supply it.

She recites the same verse when we help hold the skeins of wool that she turns into balls of yarn for knitting, when the embroidery thread tangles, when we can't find the piece we want for the jigsaw puzzle. After a while, we recite the verse along with her.

~ ~ ~

Grandfather needs an extra hired hand for a day or two. He takes me with him when he drives the ten miles to Lowe Farm. He stops the car in front of the general store where several men are gathered. Grandfather greets them, offers them work. They look at their feet. Finally one man says, *Jim if we work for you, we lose our dole.*

~ ~ ~

When we arrive home, Grandfather finds Grandmother in the kitchen. *I don't like it, Nora,* he tells her. *It's not right when I can't hire a man to do an honest day's work for an honest day's wage.* He pulls his overalls over his great long legs, laces on his heavy work boots, strides off to make sure the hired men complete all the necessary chores properly.

~ ~ ~

When a cow is calving, John Gunn stays in the barn until the calf is born. It is even more exciting when one of the mares foals. *Money in the bank,* Mother says one morning after a colt arrives safely. It is a horse colt and everyone laughs at my idea of naming him Star, which seems no funnier to me than the toothbrushes on the dog's birthday cake. I protest the adult insensitivity with a flood of tears.

~ ~ ~

Sometimes, when Grandmother and Grandfather entertain dinner guests, Grandfather puts me up on the icebox in the kitchen where I recite "Little Orphan Annie".

~ ~ ~

Going to Winnipeg is almost as exciting as Christmas.

Grandfather says it is a waste to drive all that way into the city when Eaton's would deliver the same things for free on the train.

Mother says some things, like shoes, need to be tried on.

We study the Eaton catalogue before we write our shopping list. When we get to the department store on Portage Avenue, we pretty much know what we are going to buy and what it is going to look like.

Eaton's shoe department has a special machine that allows us to see the bones in our feet, right through the new shoes. The salesman assures Mother that the shoes are a perfect fit. She looks into the viewfinder and agrees that our feet have adequate room to grow.

We always get dressed up to go to the city. When it is cold, Mother wears her Persian lamb coat. Barbara and I wear our best taffeta hair bows, dresses with matching panties or our wool plaid skirts, depending on the weather. Jim has to wear his corduroy breeches, a white shirt, and a tie, no matter what.

We lunch in Eaton's Tea Room. We order French fries served with lots of salt and malt vinegar. The waiter keeps our glasses filled with iced water. When we finish eating, the waiter brings us little glass bowls filled with warm water and a slice of lemon floating in it. We dip the tips of our fingers into the bowls, wipe our fingers on our linen napkins, dab at the corners of our mouths.

Mother takes us into the bathroom after lunch. *You need to urinate after drinking all that water,* she says. *You need to finish cleaning your hands and face,* she says. *We are not done shopping yet,* she says.

We usually see a movie while we are in the city. If Grandmother comes with us, we see a show with Will Rogers or one with Nelson Eddie and Jeanette MacDonald. When Grandmother doesn't come with us we see movies like *Stella Dallas* or *Cyclops.*

On the long ride home, I fall asleep in the back seat between Jim, Barbara and the packages, happy in the knowledge that we are bringing Grandmother a big supply of good, new string.

~ ~ ~

We make a special trip into Winnipeg just to see Walt Disney's, Snow White and the Seven Dwarfs. We don't go to Eaton's, the dentist, or anywhere. We just go to the theater, just to see the movie.

I do not sit down during the entire showing of the film. I always knew fairy tales were real, and now, Snow White, her handsome prince, her seven dwarfs, and the wicked queen perform their magic in a real movie before my very eyes.

~ ~ ~

Hoping to find ground water, Grandfather hires a dowser. After tromping around the farm all day, the dowser puts the fork cut from a willow tree branch back into the trunk of his car. *No water here, no sense in digging a well,* he tells Grandfather.

Grandfather would like to end our dependency on the cistern in the basement that collects rain water and snow melt. The cistern provides our only source of water with which we wash our clothes, ourselves, our food, and our dishes. We also make coffee, tea, lemonade and ginger beer with it.

A little hand pump brings the water up from the basement and puts it right into the kitchen sink.

~ ~ ~

Before Monday's breakfast, Tina helps Mother pump up water to heat on the kitchen stove. After breakfast, they take the hot water back down to the basement and/then pour it into the washing machine and two rinse tubs. Before they can begin washing clothes, one of the hired men starts the gasoline engine that powers the agitator in the washing machine. The engine mutters along sending out whispers of blue smoke. Grandmother uses a stout wooden pole to guide the clothes, making sure they don't tangle with the agitator's back-and-forth motion. When Grandmother decides the clothes are clean, Mother or Tina turns the crank on a big wringer mounted on the back of the washing machine, squeezing the clothes into the waiting tub of rinse water. The wringer can be dangerous, Grandmother says. It has a release spring for safety's sake, she says. I stand far away to avoid being caught in its fearsome rollers.

When the water in the first rinse tub gets too soapy, Mother unplugs the washing machine allowing the water to spill into a drain in the basement floor. She and Tina move the rinse water in the first tub into the washing machine, push the tub used for the second rinse close to the washing machine where it is used as the first rinse. Tina brings down fresh hot water for the second tub of rinse water.

Mother and Grandmother make the laundry soap themselves. The soap we wash our bodies with is bought at Eaton's.

The white clothes get washed first, the men's work clothes last.

Monday is washday, rain or shine. If it rains, the clothes hang on wooden drying racks in the basement and kitchen. Grandmother lets me hang the socks on the lowest part of the drying racks.

If it is sunny, the clothes hang on the clothesline in the back yard. *Clothes smell best when they dry outside*, Mother says.

In the winter the clothes freeze on the line. If a wind comes up before they dry, Mother and Tina rush to bring the frozen clothes into the house. They melt, leaving puddles of water under the drying racks. If the wind breaks them, the tears have to be mended and that makes more work. *Heaven knows we don't need any more work around here*, Grandmother says.

The drain in the basement takes away the dirty wash water and stores it in a covered holding tank close to the garden. An old hand pump marks the cover of the tank. When the tank gets full, Grandfather pays us a penny to pump the water out into a little ditch that irrigates the vegetable garden, utilizing every last precious drop.

~ ~ ~

On Tuesday, all the clothes from Monday's wash need to be ironed. The ironing takes place in the kitchen where the irons are heated on the stove, which makes the kitchen really hot in summer. In winter, moisture driven from the clothes steams all the windows. I would draw pictures or make designs on the windows but it makes the windows streaky.

Nerta Miller irons her sheets and tea towels. *No need for that* Grandmother says, as she folds the linens fresh from the line. Folding the tea towels has to be done correctly. Corners must match exactly before a crease is smoothed down the middle. Repeated matching and smoothing make the towels stack neatly in a kitchen drawer. I am allowed to help fold the tea towels. Folding the sheets requires the size and strength of women.

The table linens must be ironed without a wrinkle and ironed dry. Mother continues to iron while Grandmother and Tina prepare the noon meal. That way, no extra fuel is needed because both ironing and cooking get done at the same time.

When Mother needs a rest, she lets me iron the linen handkerchiefs because I know how to match corners properly.

~ ~ ~

Spring marks the beginning of preparation for the winter to come. The brooder house, taken out of its winter storage in the implement shed, signals the first step of readiness. One of the hired men scrubs down and whitewashes the little building. He completes his job by covering the floor with a bed of sawdust making the brooder house ready for its newest brood of chicks.

The awaited call comes from the railway depot at Kane. The order from the hatchery in Winnipeg has arrived. A hired man hurriedly drives to the depot to bring back the precious cargo of day-old chicks. He delivers the chirping boxes to Grandmother's and Mother's capable hands.

Small, elevated kerosene heaters warm the little brooder house. Mother treats the drinking water with an antiseptic that turns the water a lovely pale violet. She places water in special containers that look like upside down fruit jars resting in saucers.

Finally the boxes are placed on the floor. Each chick is taken out and inspected. Mother allows us to help. Grandmother and Mother, intent on making sure the chicks are healthy, do not notice that before we hand them a chick we anesthetize it. We cup the chick in our hands. Then we carefully put the chick's head in our mouth, closing our lips around its neck. We wait until it stops moving. Satisfied it is sleeping, we hold the limp body in our hands until it wakens. Then we deliver the resurrected chick to either Mother or Grandmother.

These bits of yellow fluff will turn into more eggs than we can eat, chicken for Sunday's sumptuous summer suppers, canned chicken to see us through the long winter.

~ ~ ~

Every spring at exactly the right time, Grandfather decides which fields to plant in wheat, oats, barley, alfalfa, or flax, which fields to leave fallow, which fields to put into hay, and which fields to use for pasture. Then the men begin spring planting. The horses are teamed up, hitched to the disking machine, the rake, the harrow, and then the planter. These great animals enjoy extra provisions of grain for their hard work in the fields.

~ ~ ~

When the men finish their work, the whole farm looks as if each field had been freshly ironed. Then the men begin to prepare for the Carman Fair.

Jim helps repaint the pony buggy a shiny black, the wheels fire engine red. He helps dress the leather seat to match the buggy chassis. He enters Fly in the pony division. They win a red ribbon and lead the Grand Parade the final night of the fair.

The men spend a lot of time getting a team of horses ready to show. They usually choose Maude and Turk to represent Grandfather's ability to breed Clydesdales. Maude and Ted work well together; have the same markings; arch their necks without needing a checkrein when they pull a grain wagon. After the men trim and polish Maude's and Turk's hooves like pairs of Sunday shoes, they weave a million little red rosettes into their manes and tails. They dress the harness to look like new. Maude and Ted win a red ribbon at the fair because they look exactly like the Clydesdale horses in Grandfather's book.

Grandfather spends most of his time working with the new young bull whose stud fees will reflect his ability to compete well in all the cattle shows, starting with the fair in Carman. Under Grandfather's guidance, the men confine this huge docile beast to a barn stall that is full of fresh clean straw. The straw comes up to the bull's belly to immobilize him, soften his body, give him a smooth square shape without lumps of muscle.

Grandfather takes the young bull out of the stall every day. Taking him by a new leather halter, Grandfather slowly leads the placid animal around in a circle. He talks softly while holding the bull's head so that the neck muscles ripple into the shoulder. With his cane, Grandfather coaxes the bull into planting his front feet properly to maximize the squareness of his chest, set his rear feet correctly to provide a level back which emphasizes the squareness of the rump. Grandfather judges at cattle shows. He knows exactly how to maneuver the animal, emphasize its perfection and magnify its gentle nature.

While the men clean the stall, bed it with new straw, Grandfather and John Gunn curry and brush the young bull. They clean, trim, file, wax and polish his hooves, polish his brass nose ring until it shines. Grandfather has more than pride riding on this animal's prospects of another championship.

Once, accidentally, Mother finds Barbara holding the bull by his nose ring while the men groom him, which is far worse than if she had discovered Barbara trying to milk a cow.

Grandfather's bull has one of the prettiest ribbons of all the animals at the fair. On closing night, he joins all the animals with red ribbons to parade around the racetrack. Barbara and I, seated high in the grandstand, watch the Grand Parade proudly. When Grandfather's prize bull walks past resplendent with his huge blue ribbon, his scrotum stirs up little eddies of dust in the track.

Well, Ring-a-ding-a-ding-dang-do, Barbara says as the bull and his little eddies plod serenely by.

At the fair, we don't spend much time on the midway where girls with sunburned chests wriggle and shake their grass-type hula skirts and for a dime, the barker says, you can go inside and really see them dance, or buy a real hot dog, or win a prize by knocking over stacked milk bottles, or ride on the Ferris wheel and Loop-the-Loop for five cents. Although I would dearly love to ride one of the wooden horses on the merry-go-round, *it is not necessary*, Grandmother says. *We have a pony to ride anytime we want, at home.*

Grandmother and Mother win red ribbons at the fair because they iron linen tablecloths and napkins better than anyone else.

At the fair, Uncle Jim Miller races his sulky horses in the afternoon. We probably don't go to the track to watch him race his horses for the same reason we never play cards on Sunday.

~ ~ ~

Mr. George owns the butcher shop in Roland. We have trouble understanding him when he speaks. Grandmother says that is because he is a Cockney from England. Jim says it is because the only tooth Mr. George owns hangs down from the middle of his mouth and makes him talk funny. Grandmother says, *Polite people don't stare.*

Grandmother stops in Roland to buy Mr. George's lunchmeats because they are the best, she says. The floor, covered in fresh sawdust, gives the butcher shop a just-been-built smell.

Mr. George takes a big sausage of bologna from the meat case. He uses a special machine to slice the bologna evenly. He gives each of us a slice, for free, while Grandmother places her order. Jim says the sausage is really bull meat, but he doesn't say it loud enough for anyone except Barbara and me to hear.

Every Christmas Mr. George presents Grandmother with a meat pie he makes himself. Mother says you can't tell if the pie is hot or cold because Mr. George uses so many spices. Mother lets me eat a little slice of pie after it has been heated in the oven.

~ ~ ~

The currant bushes produce the only fruit grown on the farm. The sour little berries require a lot of sugar before Mother turns them into jelly.

~ ~ ~

Every summer, two bearded, black-clad, Hutterite men come around in their old truck which is filled with fresh fruit. Mother deals with them because Grandmother doesn't like to bargain.

Mother insists that the young Hutterite show her the bottom of the basket of fruit before she makes a purchase. She trades an old sheepskin that has been in the rafters of the implement shed for a basket of Concord grapes. The young Hutterite confers with the old Hutterite in German before each deal is consummated. The old Hutterite never moves from his perch on the passenger's seat in the truck. Before they drive away, he tells Mother that she drives a hard bargain.

Mother buys baskets of Concord grapes from the Hutterites to make jelly. She also buys peaches and berries which we eat after we cover the washed fruit with sugar and cream. I like the berries the best because they make patterns in the cream.

Don't play with your food, Mother says.

~ ~ ~

Grandmother buys a Servel refrigerator. It runs on kerosene. People come from miles around to view this marvelous machine. Grandmother shows each visitor the ice cubes the refrigerator makes. She never tells anyone the ice tastes faintly of kerosene.

Still, if we want to make ice cream, we have to go to Kane, where ice, cut and hauled by sled from the river in winter, is stored in a special shed then covered in heaps of sawdust. On the hottest day, the cool shed smells like Victoria Beach. The ice, which lasts all summer, is terribly expensive.

When Mother makes ice cream, it means important guests have been invited to dinner.

~ ~ ~

Grandmother does not allow me to say, *I can't*. She only allows me to say, *I don't know how*. Then she knows what to teach me she says.

If I say, I don't care, Grandmother sternly recites.

Don't Care was made to care

Don't Care was hung

Don't Care was put in a pot

and stewed 'til he was done.

~ ~ ~

Ever since Sandy, our ex-house cat, deserted us, it is necessary to set traps for the little field mice when they sneak into the house to look for a safe winter home. Barbara, terrified of mice, coaxes me to empty the traps in the attic. *You are smaller and can get in the corners better,* she tells me.

After collecting several of the little dead mice, I decide to give them a ride in my doll buggy. Upon discovering the latest addition to my doll collection, Grandmother, unaffected by my tearful pleas, insists I throw the little dead mice away.

Barbara sits practicing music Mother brought from Winnipeg especially for her. The score has a picture of Snow White and the Seven Dwarfs on the cover. I find a piece of string and drag it across Barbara's neck. She leaps straight into the air, screaming and shrieking. Mother rushes in, administers resounding smacks to my thighs, while trying to calm Barbara at the same time.

Grandmother, surveying the scene, says *Shame, shame* to me.

I am the only person ever to believe it was only a piece of string, not a dead mouse's tail that I dragged across Barbara's neck.

~ ~ ~

On the way into Winnipeg, Grandfather drives the car. Grandmother sits in the passenger's seat. I listen to the discussion about my sore tooth from the isolation of the backseat.

Grandmother says she thinks a filling will fix the tooth as good as new. Grandfather says he thinks fillings cost too much money, pulling the tooth takes care of the problem once and for all. Grandmother says she thinks the dentist will know what is best for the tooth.

The conversation turns to crops, the weather, the price of wheat and cattle. Grandmother wonders if we should plan to eat in Winnipeg. Grandfather thinks we shouldn't make plans until after the visit to the dentist.

In the office, the dentist explains the health benefits of filling the tooth as opposed to extracting it. Cost is the deciding factor.

I do not relinquish my tooth without a struggle.

~ ~ ~

The front porch steps conceal a hiding place, and I am the only one who knows about it. Well, not the only one---a rabbit has been there, but he is no longer around. The secret spot is mine. The entrance, hidden by the spirea bushes, assures my privacy, my freedom from detection.

A shrill blast from Mother's police whistle destroys my illusion of invisibility. A call from her whistle means I am to stop whatever I am doing and hurry to her as quickly as possible, a rule she will not tolerate being broken.

I ponder the demand to respond. I decide to ignore this seemingly unreasonable rule, lean back, enjoy the cool quiet of my secret domain.

My serenity is short lived. The blast from Mother's whistle becomes longer and louder. Soon Jim and Barbara are walking rapidly around the house, calling and looking for me. Tina has been sent to the garden to investigate. Mother continues blowing her whistle while she combs the windbreak. I watch the parade of legs go past my sanctuary.

Suddenly, without warning, the bushes part, and Grandmother's face appears at the entrance of my little cave. *Come out of there*, she says. I am surprised how much she sounds like Grandfather. She summons Mother.

Mother red-faced and teary-eyed, grabs me in a tight hug before she covers my thighs with sharp slaps from her open hand. I have frightened her badly and I am truly sorry she has to spank me so much to prove it.

~ ~ ~

Instead of going to Victoria Beach, we spend the summer in Rapid City. Auntie Edna has taken the basement apartment in Dr. Beebe's home. Dr. Beebe, a professor at the School of Mines, and his family will be gone for the summer. We take care of their place in return for living in their basement.

We never go anywhere, ever.

I invent peanut butter and syrup sandwiches. First I toast the bread, spread peanut butter generously on one side, put the other slice of toasted bread over the peanut buttered slice, generously butter the top slice of toast, carefully pour just the exact correct amount of syrup in the middle of the sandwich. I mop up all the syrup by cutting the sandwich into neat little squares properly using a knife and fork.

Jim finds the concoction disgusting.

I find that making and eating the sandwiches helps relieve the tedium.

Toward the end of our stay, Lewis Beebe, Dr. Beebe's teen-age son, opens the door to our apartment by mistake, excuses himself and leaves.

I think he must be the handsome prince sent to rescue me from my subterranean jail.

I wait and wait for his return.

Eventually we pack up and go back to the farm.

~~~

After much discussion and careful consideration, Mother decides that we will live in the United States for a whole year with Auntie Edna.

We head south in the Plymouth, carefully packed by Grandmother. The journey begins with Grandfather driving.

Mother sits in the passenger's seat. We sit carefully in the back seat. We cross the line.

I have been across the border before. I know there is no line, just a building where we will be stopped and asked some questions by men in khaki uniforms.

Because Mother has all our necessary papers, we are not detained at American customs.

As we travel leisurely on the dusty gravel road, Grandfather inspects the crops. He drives on the shoulder of the right side of the road, then on the shoulder of the left side of the road. The crops pass inspection until we get close to the Missouri River where the soil has taken on a strange pale reddish color.

When Grandfather becomes tired from driving and crop inspections, he lets Mother take the wheel.

We know we are in a foreign country when we read the road signs. Shiver my timbers, cried Captain Mac, we're ten miles out, but we're going back,I forgot my Burma Shave. Another sign reads, Said Juliet to Romeo, if you don't shave, go homeo, Burma Shave.

Little signs elevated on stakes announce the miles to Wall Drug Store, Wall, South Dakota. They also promise a glass of ice water.

When at last we reach Wall, Mother pulls off the highway and on to the street where the anticipated drug store sits. We really do get a free glass of ice water.

Grandfather gives us a lesson in American English. The state capital of South Dakota is pronounced Peer.

Obviously, no French live in South Dakota.

He tells us how to pronounce garage, schedule, laboratory, and aluminum correctly.

You're going to be Americans now, he tells us.

The day stays hot, dry, and dusty.

After several sightings of cactus, Mother wonders aloud why she decided to move to the desert.

~ ~ ~

When we arrive in Rapid City, I feel uncomfortable in the new surroundings. No matter how many times I run outdoors, houses, trees, and hills are all I can see. When the sun sets, it quickly flops behind a mountain to end the day. On the prairie, twilight takes a long, long time to fade into night.

~ ~ ~

In Rapid City, I am introduced to strangers as Miss Davidson's niece.

~ ~ ~

Edna says if I don't stop walking like a duck, she will have me put in braces. It is six blocks to school, six blocks back. I watch my feet every step of the way, concentrating on their correct placement.

~ ~ ~

School confuses me. The entire classroom at Woodrow Wilson Elementary School is filled with fifth grade students and when Miss Stordahl introduces me, she uses the word foreigner.

At recess time the children gather around me, only to be disappointed that I speak English, came to Rapid City in a car, have never seen the ocean nor met the Dionne quintuplets.

Spelling and math lessons present special problems. Miss Stordahl puts big red check marks after I write cheque, colour, and theatre on my spelling tests.

She says the way I write fractions is incorrect.

I come home complaining to Auntie Edna about the strange words being used when we sing "God Save the King".

~ ~ ~

School is over for the summer. We return to the farm. Everything is the same, except Rex and Fly are no longer there.

After we moved away, Rex wouldn't eat or move from his mat in the dining room. John Gunn took him out behind the windbreak and shot him.

Fly has been sold.

It is a working farm and we know animals that don't earn their keep are expendable.

~ ~ ~

Mother goes into Winnipeg to spend a lot of time at the American consulate.

She is trying to get papers for us to live in the United States permanently.

The name of the man in charge is Bernard Heiler.

Mother does not like Mr. Heiler.

No matter how many papers she brings him, he always sends her home again.

Canada is at war, he tells her.

Not with the United States, Mother tells him back.

Mr. Heiler doesn't care. He says she still needs more papers.

Edna comes up from Rapid City.

We all drive the long fifty miles into Winnipeg.

We spend the day sharing a small reception room in the consulate with a Norwegian sailor.

The sailor is also seeking asylum in the United States.

Mr. Heiler won't let the sailor into the United States, either.

We don't like the way Mr. Heiler looks.

He is short, has dirty fingernails, wears a badly ironed white shirt, and ill-fitting gray pants.

Jim says Mr. Heiler looks like he is having a baby in the back of his pants.

Mother comes out of Mr. Heiler's office to tell us to be quiet: we will be leaving soon.

On the way back to the farm, Auntie Edna says she is going to report Mr. Heiler to the Justice Department when she gets back to Rapid City.

Maybe she did because shortly afterward, we are issued permanent visas.

We return to the United States forever.

Part 3:
Being, Becoming, and Behaving
American 1939–1947

Rapid City, gateway to the Black Hills of South Dakota, boasts a population of 11364 and two hospitals.

Auntie Edna runs the Black Hills Methodist Hospital.

The Sisters run Saint John's.

Part of Auntie Edna's hospital is old and built of wood. The other part is new and built of sandstone.

Saint John's is all new and built of brick.

The lobby in Auntie Edna's hospital is dark.

The lobby in Saint John's has a painted statue of Jesus with a big red heart on the outside of his robe.

The Sisters wear a veil and wimple to protect them from the world.

Auntie Edna wears a wall of heavily corseted fat to protect her from the world.

When the sheriff arrests someone suffering from alcohol poisoning, he brings the prisoner to Auntie Edna's hospital one time, the Sister's hospital the next.

Sometimes Auntie Edna tells us about the interesting cases before the information is printed in the *Rapid City Daily Journal*—like when cowboys have a shootout at a Saturday night dance in Hermosa.

~ ~ ~

Rapid Creek divides Rapid City into two parts. The poor people and Indians live on the north side of the creek; the rest of us live on the south side of the creek.

~ ~ ~

The Rose Marketeria, the best grocery store in town, delivers groceries, just like Eaton's does in Winnipeg. The deliveryman for the Rose brings the groceries in a truck. Eaton's delivers their groceries in a van driven by a man in livery, pulled by a matched pair of Clydesdales, one of whom was born on our farm.

~ ~ ~

On Saturday mornings, in Rapid City, Mother gives Jim the grocery list, along with the five dollars she has for grocery money. It takes all three of us to get the little red wagon to the Rose Marketeria. There, one of the grocery clerks takes Mother's list, loads the required items into our wagon. We haul the week supply of groceries home to Mother who is waiting for her exact change.

The Marketeria enjoys the reputation of having the best butcher in Rapid City. Mother doesn't think much of him. She says he sells round steak by the yard.

~ ~ ~

For entertainment, we telephone the Rose Marketeria to ask if they have Prince Albert in the can. Let him out before he drowns, we yell into the ear of the startled grocery clerk.

The Rex Theater, one of three movie theaters, offers a Saturday matinee. For a dime, I can see a serial, the latest Pathe newsreel and two cowboy movies. The early audience at the Rex is mostly kids. No self-respecting high schooler would ever go there.

Discarded Coke bottles, returned to the neighborhood store for their redemption fee, supply my Saturday movie money.

Neither Auntie Edna nor Mother will contribute to the trashy movie fare shown at the Rex Theater.

They pay my way to films they approve of. The Elk Theater shows the best films. In this nicer house, I view *The Wizard of Oz, Gone with the Wind,* and *Jessie James.*

~ ~ ~

Saturday is the best day to shop in Rapid City. Working people get off at noon. They take advantage of the specials the merchants offer to lure ranchers and their families in town to purchase staples.

The best stores line St. Joe Street. Sorbel's offers the nicest ladies shoes. F&M stocks fine boots. Barons provides the latest in ladies wear. When some of the wealthier ladies come in the shop, the seamstress who does alterations quickly sews a smaller dress size into the dresses to be presented for their approval and possible purchase.

The best bars on St. Joe do a brisk business, especially on Saturday. The School of Mines students hang out at the Brass Rail or the Anchor if they have a spare dime for a glass of beer. Tired businessmen meet before going back for the late closing of their stores and people drop in after seeing a movie at the Elk Theater.

Main Street on Saturday night enjoys a carnival atmosphere. Indians come in from the Rosebud and Pine Ridge reservations. During tourist season, Peter Duhamel pays some of the Indians to dance in front of his trading post on Sixth Street. Tourists gather around to watch. Townspeople pay no mind to the diversion.

The cowboys, some of whom are Indians, are in town to play. Rich with a month's pay, the white cowboys frequent the bars on Main Street where they can dance, drink, and find the easy women.

The real Saturday night action takes place in front of the liquor store on the corner of Sixth and Main.

A white man waits for an Indian cowboy to approach him. For a tidy sum, the white man purchases a half pint of cheap whiskey inside the store, returns, slips the forbidden bottle to the waiting Indian.

Quickly unscrewing the cap, the Indian cowboy consumes the entire contents of the little bottle in one long swallow. If he is still standing after a few minutes, he sends the white man back into the store for another small, expensive bottle of cheap whiskey. This time, the semi conscious Indian steadies himself on the nearest lamppost, tilts up the bottle, and slugs it down. He bravely flirts with alcohol poisoning to avoid arrest.

No one seems to mind, except the sheriff. Federal law not withstanding, he doesn't want another dead Indian in his jail.

Instead, he takes his unconscious prisoner to one of the hospitals.

～～～

Sunday Main Street is quiet when Auntie Edna takes us to the Virginia Café after church.

～～～

On the first day of May we make little baskets of construction paper. After school we fill the baskets with grass, a wild flower, or a piece of candy. We leave the love offering on a carefully chosen doorstep, ring the doorbell, and then hide. Everyone is genuinely surprised by their unexpected treat, especially Mother.

～～～

Going to school in the sixth grade seems to make me sick a lot. Mr. Roth, the teacher, has thinning hair, picks his nose and farts into the hot air vent. He gives me an A for Ingenuity. It is the only good grade I receive the entire year.

During one of my absences from school, I stumble onto a book of Greek mythology. The outrageous behavior of the gods and goddesses dumbfounds me. These stories are a far cry from the ones Grandmother read to us from *Hulbert's Children's Stories of the Bible.* z

I discuss my new-found knowledge with no one. *True Romance* and *True Detective* can't hold a candle to these stories and Auntie Edna says, *True Romance and True Detective* are trash magazines.

～～～

When I smoke a cigarette, I make the best smoke rings of anyone in the sixth grade.

～～～

Mother applies for a job as hostess at the Virginia Café because the sign in one of the café's windows says they need one. Because times are hard the management only hires Americans, Mother learns.

Three weeks later the sign still rests in the window.

～～～

The dreaded little red wagon sits in the middle of the living room floor which means we are moving again.

Every time we move, I pack the wagon with Auntie Edna's books, magazines, the contents of the bathroom cabinets, pots and pans from the kitchen.

I drag the wagon back and forth between the house we are vacating and the house we are moving into. Auntie Edna pays me a nickel a wagon load.

Sometimes the weather is hot. Sometimes Auntie Edna is in tears. Sometimes Mother is there to help. Sometimes she has gone away again.

～～～

Auntie Edna subscribes to the Community Concert Series by purchasing four tickets.

Over the years I listen to Yehudi Menhuin play his violin, John Sebastian play classical music, including Claire de Lune, on his harmonica, Paul Robeson sing, "There is a Balm in Gilead" and recite the Moore's closing soliloquy in Othello, spend an evening listening to a string quartet, and watch the elegance of ballet.

Edna also subscribes to The Book of the Month Club.

I wish to God she'd pay the rent, is Mother's evaluation of Auntie Edna's earnest efforts to expose us to culture

~ ~ ~

Edna, no longer able to tolerate Mother's raging libido, manages to wrangle an appointment with the only psychiatrist in the state. She drives Mother the four hundred miles necessary for a session with this learned Freudian analyst.

After they waited in his reception room for an impressive period of time, a nurse ushers Mother into the hush of his inner office. When she is properly seated, the doctor asks how her sex life is.

It's wonderful, is her reply, *how's yours?*

He immediately dismisses her.

Auntie Edna and Mother return home. Auntie, voicing disdain for the art of psychiatry, bemoans Mother's continuing wayward ways.

~ ~ ~

Georgia Rowe introduces me to her mother. *Why, Georgia,* Mrs. Rowe says, *This is the little girl who always looks at her feet.*

Mrs. Rowe learns that I like to read. She gives me a book about Elsie Dinsmore. The heroine, motherless Elsie, suffers from unrealistic expectations about obedience. Rather than play the piano on the Sabbath, which she considers work, or disobey Papa, Elsie faints and hits her head on the piano.

I return the book quickly with the remark that Elsie is the dumbest sap I ever read about.

Mrs. Rowe stiffens, the tick around her left eye making her grimace more wildly than ever.

What are you reading now, dear? she inquires.

Gone With the Wind, I reply enthusiastically.

~ ~ ~

Immersed in *Gone With the Wind*, a certain passage confuses me. I seek out Edna for clarification.

Auntie, what does rape mean? I ask.

It's when a man forces his attentions on a woman, she replies.

I reread the paragraph. *Why would a man want to kiss a woman who doesn't want to kiss him back?* I ask my maiden aunt, who offers no further insight into the puzzling behavior of courtship.

~ ~ ~

A cool early morning in June, Mother deposits me on a seat behind the bus driver. She shows him my ticket, tucks it into my suitcase, then tucks the suitcase under my seat.

She admonishes the driver: I am to remain seated directly behind him at all times.

The driver gives Mother a knowing nod.

She kisses me goodbye and disembarks all the while assuring me that I will be fine until Grandfather picks me up in Morden.

The bus meanders from Rapid City, across the Missouri River, north through the Red River valley.

I stay seated directly behind the bus driver. Even when there is a change of bus driver, my placement on the bus remains the same.

Hours and hours and hours later, Grandfather picks me up in Morden, puts my suitcase in the back seat while I climb into the passenger's seat. We drive the thirty miles to the farm in silence. Grandfather inspects the crops by driving first on the right shoulder of the road, then on the left shoulder of the road.

The prairie from Morris to Kane is a sea of green wheat, oats, and barley.

The wind gives whispery promises of another generous harvest.

~ ~ ~

When we arrive at the farm, Grandmother greets me at the door, takes me to a bedroom and leaves me to unpack. After a little lunch I wander around until suppertime.

Everything has changed.

The Clydesdales and their tack have been sold.

Only Ted and Maude remain for the impending harvest.

No cattle graze the raggedy pastures.

The hen house, un-white washed and free of dusty feed and oyster shells, produces silence.

The empty hog pens have allowed the pig wallow to dry up.

The hay meadows lie fallow.

The only acreage planted in wheat is that which Grandfather and his one hired hand will be able to harvest.

The house garden sprouts one row of Grandmother's beloved gladiola, nothing more.

John Gunn had promised to stay on the farm to help Grandfather grow wheat for the war effort. After the Germans bomb Edinburgh, John joins the Canadian Air Force. Not much later he will die in a training accident.

The hired men who had always worked for us are gone away, too.

Even Tina doesn't work for Grandmother anymore.

~ ~ ~

George Miller comes into the kitchen, too upset to accept Grandmother's offer of fresh coffee.

What's going on with this country, Jim, he demands of my grandfather. *I planted sugar beets because the government said we need them for the war effort. They promised me help; I don't know anything about growing sugar beets. Do you know who they sent me on the train yesterday? They sent me a Japanese man and his wife. He's a college professor. His little wife is terrified of the country; she's some kind of a musician. What am I supposed to do with them and these beets I have in the ground?* He storms out of the kitchen, climbs into his Buick, leaves a rooster tail of dust in the lane that leads to the main road.

~~~

The Red Cross has given Grandmother mounds of Air Force blue yarn; she uses some of it to teach me how to knit socks, my contribution to the war effort, she says. Uncle Jim Miller has already knit a hundred pairs. She tells me this to encourage me.

After morning chores of bed-making and breakfast dishes, we begin my sock-building lesson.

The first requirement to knit a sock is that a certain number of stitches be cast onto three individual needles. Somehow yarn connects the needles, magically making a circle. With a little sleight of hand, a fourth needle is brought into play and the cuff of the sock begins. Knit two, purl two, knit two, purl two until all three needles have been knitted around to establish the pattern. The skilled knitter ends up with purl two as the last two stitches. The same procedure continues until the cuff reaches three inches in length. Then the pattern requires only the knitting stitch for several inches.

Turning the heel provides the next challenge.

My attempt to master yet another knitting technique proves unsuccessful. The yarn becomes frayed from endless unraveling.

I use hired hand language when Grandmother isn't looking because she can read lips even if she can't hear me.

Eventually, Grandmother tires of my struggle. She turns the heel for me.

I then knit the foot, which is sort of like the leg, except now I start to decrease for the toe.

To decrease, two stitches are knit together in an orderly fashion until only a few stitches remain to be cast off.

This means I have created a sock.

Grandmother, unable to knit and read at the same time, allows the radio to be played.

We listen to the soap opera, *Old Ma Perkins*. She sells New Improved Oxydol Laundry Soap on the radio. Listening to her trials and tribulations is supposed to distract us from the discomfort of knitting during the summer heat and humidity. Grandmother reminds me about string and knots and patience.

～～～

The grain ripens. Grandfather takes me away from knitting and into the fields to drive the grain wagon to the elevator in Kane. Grandfather uses a combine this year, a machine that needs only two men to operate it.

The combine picks up the mowed grain, scatters the straw on the field and shoots the grain into a hopper. When the hopper is full, I drive Ted and Maude alongside the combine, a mechanism lowers the chute, the hopper empties into the wagon, the combine continues on, pulled by Grandfather driving the John Deere tractor. After the wagon fills, I listen to Grandfather's admonitions.

Mind you drive the horses slowly, Grandfather says. *Mind you take the corner onto the main road nice and wide,* he says. *Don't hurry,* he says. *The horses know the way,* he says. *The man at the elevator is expecting you, he'll help you unload the wagon,* he says. *Be careful,* he says, as I drive the team away.

Roy Welch no longer runs the grain elevator. The man in charge makes me get down from the wagon. I stand far away against a wall while he dumps the grain into the huge storage bins.

The wind from the dumping grain throws clouds of chaff high into the air.

Maude, Ted, and I drive the mile back to the waiting combine and its wheat-filled hopper.

Grandfather comes in from the fields grey with fatigue. We eat supper in silence. Grandmother is too tired and I am too old for the reading of a bedtime story.

~ ~ ~

About two weeks before the fall school term begins, Barbara arrives at the farm. She has been released from her kitchen duties at the Black Hills General Hospital where she spent a lot of time peeling potatoes, using a special machine housed in the basement.

Jim makes too much money working at the cement plant to take a holiday before school starts.

Grandmother takes us into Winnipeg to outfit us for school with proper leather shoes, wool plaid skirts, blouses and wool sweaters to see us through a cold Dakota winter.

She puts us aboard the bus at Morden, armed with sandwiches, fruit and a bottle of water secured with a newly developed bottle top that will stop any size bottle neck.

The stopper, a complicated mechanism involving rubber and stainless steel, must be twisted correctly for it to fit securely into the bottle. Our supply of water is thus secured in an ex-ginger ale bottle.

The trip begins and I become thirsty. An argument ensues. Barbara says it is a long way before we will be able to get any more water and I should wait before I drink any.

When she isn't looking, I uncork the bottle, sneak a swig, and put the stopper back into the bottle incorrectly. Water rolls out from under our seats and all the way to the back of the bus.

Barbara gets up and moves far away from me.

I ride without her company the rest of the long, long trip back to Rapid City.

~ ~ ~

Mickey Jackson, Dr. Jackson's second wife, wears big diamonds and fur coats, plays bridge, and always invites us over for Thanksgiving dinner.

She gets up at 4:00 a.m. to start the turkey.

No one can cook a turkey like Mickey Jackson, Auntie Edna says.

Mickey used to be Kate McKee, a Canadian and a nurse before she married the doctor.

~ ~ ~

After listening to my complaints while Mother picks gravel out of my knee, Auntie Edna brings home a pair of roller skates.

Rollerskating requires several skills, mastery of the large skate key being the first one. One end of the key makes it possible to change the size of the skate to the same length as my shoes. The other end of the key helps me to tighten the clamps around the sole of my shoe. A leather strap, buckled across the top of my foot, completes the securing of skates to shoes.

The key, worn on a stout cord around my neck, enables me to constantly realign and tighten the skates.

Roller-skating replaces the lost joy of ice skating. I am able to remain upright on roller skates.

I skate all summer; I experience a variety of sidewalk challenges. Eighth Street proves to be the perfect grade for rollerskating, except for one block.

There the sidewalk is full of cracks, tufts of grass, dangerously shifted slabs of concrete.

Mother, occupied by other concerns, remains oblivious to my skinned hands and knees, bruised bum and thighs, broken shoes.

Eventually, I learn to navigate all of Eighth Street, jump the curbs, cross the intersections, and achieve speeds unknown when I could ice skate.

~ ~ ~

In the winter, the police barricade Sixth Street all the way down the hill to Kansas City Street. Almost everyone has a sled. Those who don't, careen down the hill on a piece of cardboard.

~ ~ ~

On the way out to visit Dr. Jackson's cabin on Canyon Lake, we drive past a field where some men are at work.

All of the men have shovels. Some dig into the ground, some lean on their shovel. There seems to be no sense of urgency among the workmen.

When I ask Auntie Edna what the men are doing, she replies, *Not much. It's a WPA project, part of the New Deal. The project gives work to unemployed men. The letters stand for We Piddle Around,* she explains giggling.

~ ~ ~

Mary Olsen, a quiet girl in the sixth grade, pesters me to go to church with her. I relent and accompany her on a Sunday morning. The church is in a dilapidated building. No spire or stained glass windows establish its authority.

I regret my decision. No music, no formally led prayers, no sermon are incorporated into the worship service. Instead, two men in shabby suits pace back and forth among the congregation, exhorting everyone to repent.

One of the men stops at the front of the room to tell the now moaning congregants about a nonbeliever who is in danger of being crushed by the reckless driver of a large truck. The nonbeliever cries out, *Jesus Christ!*

It sounds pretty much like the language I was not supposed to hear when one of the hired men was exasperated with an uncooperative animal.

Usually, *Jesus Christ* was just the beginning of the oath.

The man rushes down the aisle. He stops and stooping down to my eye level demands, Little girl, do you want to be saved?

I don't have time right now, I tell him, I have to meet my mother at the movies.

~ ~ ~

Mother tells about the winter she and Auntie Edna, Grandmother, and Grandfather separated all the wheat from the weed seeds.

They sorted bushel after bushel by lamplight.

That spring, Grandfather sold his clean wheat for top dollar.

And when the War was on, he and Mother and Auntie Edna planted and harvested all the wheat because there were no men to help.

And the time Grandfather insisted on taking his own grain to the miller and the flour he brought home wouldn't make decent bread.

Maybe that is why Mother takes too many barbiturates sometimes; to help her forget the other memories she never talks about.

~ ~ ~

I am awakened by sounds of muffled crying. I get up and trot out to the front room just in time to see Edna leading Mother out to the car. Mother is crying into her best linen and lace hanky. She is wearing her winter coat, and Auntie is carrying a small suitcase. I inquire where they are going, why Mother is crying, why are they leaving so late at night. *You get back into bed this instant,* Edna commands. I know better than to argue with that tone of voice. I return to bed.

~~~

Seated at the dinner table with several of Auntie Edna's guests, we enjoy Mother's specially prepared company meal of roast beef, mashed potatoes, fresh asparagus and fruit salad. Ester, one of the nurses from Auntie Edna's hospital, asks Jim what he wants to be when he grows up.

He stops eating, licks his fork, uses it to scratch his head, replies he that hopes to become a garbage man.

I sit, frozen in terror, waiting for Jim's inevitable destruction. The adults resume their conversation although no other guest inquires about Barbara's or my plans for the future.

~~~

Our job is to go to school, Mother says; she has her own job. If we have problems with a teacher, we are to solve them. If we get into trouble she doesn't want to hear about it. She has enough troubles of her own.

~~~

Mr. Alkyre teaches eighth-grade math. I don't understand the first concept of algebra.

Letters make words. To confuse letters with nonsensical numbers is incomprehensible.

Wearying of my questioning, Mr. Alkyre stops, raps a ruler sharply on his desk to gain the attention of the entire class. He clears his throat.

Stand up, Marion, he says.

I comply.

Class, says Mr. Alkyre, *this is Marion Bruce. She is the stupidest girl in the eighth grade. Sit down Marion.*

Mother studies my report card. *I can't understand why you get such bad grades in math,* she says. Mother comes home from work on Saturday afternoon. *I told you to clean the floor in the living room,* she says. *I did,* I insist. We end up on our hands and knees on the floor. To my surprise, the floor is still dirty.

The following Monday, after school, Dr. Newby examines my eyes, tests my vision. He prescribes glasses for me.

I now see the blackboard perfectly.

I still don't understand algebra.

~ ~ ~

When Aunt Lena, Mother's best friend, remarries, her vows to love, honor and obey include Uncle Art and his sons, Grant, Keith and John.

As a Commonwealth nation, Canada follows Great Britain into war against Germany and Italy.

Grant joins the Royal Canadian Air Force.

He is killed piloting an American lend-lease plane during the Battle of Britain.

Keith joins the Royal Canadian Air Force.

He is killed piloting an American lend-lease plane during the Battle of Britain.

When John goes to enlist, Aunt Lena accompanies him.

She explains to the recruiter that the family cannot afford another casualty in the Battle of Britain.

John goes to medical school instead.

~ ~ ~

Mother has difficulty keeping a job. Her employers love her when she is normal or high; fire her when she hurtles into the depths of her unfathomable depressions.

When Mother is well, working steadily, has a little spare money, she suggests we leave the supper dishes, go to a movie instead. She always says, *Perhaps the elves will do the dishes while we are gone.* They never do, but we always hope one time they might.

~ ~ ~

I am wakened one night. I get out of bed to investigate the sounds. I find Auntie on one side of Mother and Barbara on the other. They are in the kitchen holding Mother in an upright position. The table has been pushed aside to make more room for their slow pacing back and forth while Edna squeezes lemon juice into Mother's slack mouth.

What are you doing? I ask, now wide awake.

Go to bed! Auntie Edna says.

But what's wrong with Mother? I demand to know.

She's had an accident, Edna snarls. *Now! Get back to bed right now!*

I retreat into my bedroom. I do not manage to return to sleep until the house is quiet again and by then the sun is coming up.

~ ~ ~

Usually Barbara and I are awarded the Saturday morning cleaning chores.

Barbara takes her job seriously. She moves the furniture when she vacuums, scrubs the corners of the kitchen floor as clean as the middle, moves knickknacks aside, dusts underneath, organizes scattered newspapers, swipes the top of the door jamb free of invisible grime.

I take refuge amid the dust balls, books and magazines under Auntie Edna's bed. There I stay, feasting on copies of *The Ladies' Home Journal,*

The Atlantic Monthly, The Journal of the American Medical Association, the latest selection from the *Book of the Month Club,* until Barbara hauls me out by the leg and with a well placed swat, returns me to my despised tasks.

~ ~ ~

We move to a wonderful house, four miles from town, close to Canyon Lake. Dr. Jackson owns the property. The house sits on the edge of Rapid Creek. In the spring, we feed the wild ducks and ducklings stale bread instead of saving it for moldy bread poultices.

Dr. Jackson lets us use his canoe, hollowed from a mahogany log. He brought the canoe back from Central America when he had a coffee plantation there, before he practiced medicine in Rapid City. The canoe is unsinkable.

~ ~ ~

Mrs. Straub, uncomplainingly bent under the weight of childless widowhood, lives next door to us in a little green cabin. She works at Auntie's hospital. She is from Missouri, talks funny, wears the same dress every day. We always give her a ride to and from work.

When Barbara complains about Mrs. Straub's sucking her teeth all the way to town in the morning and all the way back home from work in the evening, Auntie Edna fixes her with a withering glare.

Mrs. Straub is the soul of kindness, Edna retorts, ending further complaints.

Mrs. Straub always says, *Thanks a million.* She possesses every Colliers magazine ever printed. After supper, I go over to her house where she lets me read her valued collection.

In the winter, she keeps her cabin warm with a little kerosene heater.

She owns a radio, her one extravagance in life. She never misses a *Fibber Magee and Molly* show or *Allen's Alley.* She thinks Bob Hope is too racy sometimes.

~ ~ ~

The Japanese bomb Pearl Harbor. Auntie Edna thinks it is time the Americans got into the war. Mother is inconsolable. *Don't cry, I* tell her. *Jim will never have to go.*

~ ~ ~

The headlines in the *Rapid City Daily Journal* announce Gene Krupa's arrest in Los Angeles for possession of marijuana.

Are they crazy in Los Angeles? I ask Auntie.

Hemp grows wild in South Dakota. The Indian kids smoke it because it is a federal offense for them to possess alcohol.

Evidently harvesting, drying and smoking certain parts of the hemp plant is more fun than fooling around with corn silk.

~ ~ ~

The old high school now serves as the junior high school and a place for band practice.

Mr. Schneider never has enough French horn players for the school band.

I happily volunteer to be a band member. I would rather sit in band practice at 7:00 a.m. than in Auntie Edna's hospital lobby waiting for school to start.

I practice the horn diligently for six weeks until Mother, manic, menopausal, and unable to endure really loud and nonsensical sounds makes me return the instrument to Mr. Schneider. Mr. Schneider decides I should trade in my French horn for a cornet.

My skills fail to improve with the change of instruments. Mother demands that I turn in my cornet. I return to Auntie Edna's hospital to wait for school to start.

I experience another failure at playing a musical instrument.

~ ~ ~

After work, in the early evening, Auntie Edna takes me to Barons. Mrs. Barons waits on us. Auntie does not like any of the coats Mrs. Barons shows us.

Don't you have something cheaper! she demands.

Mrs. Barons presents us with the ugliest gray coat I have ever seen.

Edna looks at the price tag. I'll take it, she says.

~ ~ ~

Auntie Edna works long hours at her hospital. She comes home from work too tired to eat dinner. After she has eaten several cheese sandwiches with extra butter and salt, she takes a little yellow pill. She is too tired to sleep and the little pill helps her have a restful night so that she can spend another full day at her hospital.

Edna oversees the cleaning of the old wooden part of the building where germs lie in wait. No one gets an infection in her clean hospital.

The top floor of the old hospital is reserved for the aged poor. Most of the patients are too enfeebled or demented to care for themselves. They are kept clean, well fed, and safe under minimal supervision.

Mr. Morkhort, a tall, angular, old cowboy cannot get out of bed. Short-tempered, he gets angry when someone does not respond immediately to his verbal requests for help. He will not push the call button pinned to his pillow. When he needs to use the urinal, he hollers once or twice for help before he bangs the urinal against the wall. If no one arrives in time to help, he manages to use the urinal by himself. He bangs the container against the wall to tell the nurse he is finished. Urine splashes all over the wall.

Mr. Crowly, an old rancher, speaks in a voice barely above a whisper. He rings his bell to ask for his needs to be satisfied.

His favorite request is paper and pencil with which to write his long-dead friends. He closes each letter with; "bye now, the calves is bawling". Because he has no envelopes or stamps he hands the letters to anyone who comes into the room. He is confident the letter will be mailed and delivered.

Minnie and Charlie Caton have a room to themselves. Bedridden with tertiary syphilis, they spend most of the day yelling unintelligible oaths at each other.

My job after school requires me to deliver the afternoon snacks to the old folks. All the residents smile and say *Thanks a lot,* gulp the anticipated treat of a glass of juice. All, except the Catons.

Sometimes Minnie scratches at me when I attempt to hand her the juice. Sometimes Charlie throws his juice on the floor instead of drinking it.

What makes the Catons smell so awful, I ask Auntie Edna? She responds by giving me her copy of a public health book, properly illustrated with color plates, so I can learn about venereal diseases.

After carefully studying Auntie Edna's textbook, I announce I'm not going to deliver the Catons their fruit juice, anymore.

~ ~ ~

Edna puts me to work in the room where the surgical implements are readied for the autoclave.

The nurses explain the uses of the various instruments while we clean them. Some of the instruments look like modified versions of the tools Mr. George used in his butcher shop.

~ ~ ~

The summer Barbara is sixteen, Edna assigns her to the night shift on the third floor. The war makes cheap help unavailable.

~ ~ ~

Edna, with the impaired judgment of a menopausal woman, decides to take Jim, his best friend John, my best friend Polly, and me to visit Grandmother and Grandfather in their new retirement home in Carman. The trip consists of two main events. The really exciting experience takes place in Winnipeg at Hudson Bay Department Store on Portage Avenue. Polly and I successfully race to the top of the down escalator in the grand entrance of this hallowed trading post only to be greeted by an elegantly dressed floor walker who explains that our adventure is over. The second highlight of the trip consists of surviving the unrelenting torment of Jim and John on the way back to Rapid City. They ask us to tell them what dirty words mean, tease us about our brassière sizes. Edna never again attempts to be travel guide using teen-agers as passengers.

~ ~ ~

Jim helps Otto Wolf, the only sheep rancher in West River, with lambing. He works hard in the spring cold of open range. Otto Wolf pays Jim the same wage he pays the men because he says Jim is as good at lambing as any of the men who work for him. After a successful lambing and with money in his pockets, Jim relaxes at home over a cup of Mother's fresh strong coffee. Excusing himself, he goes to the door and spits a stream of tobacco juice in the general direction of the creek. Mother jumps up from the table, takes a package of cigarettes from her carton, hands it to Jim with the admonition he is never to chew tobacco again ever in front of her or anyone else not ever.

He explains that he couldn't smoke while delivering lambs; God, he couldn't even get a cigarette lit.

You're not on the ranch now, Mother sternly reminds him.

~ ~ ~

Before Jim leaves for the ranch, he gathers homework from each teacher with the understanding he will be granted an excused absence when he turns in his completed homework. On returning to school, Jim turns in his homework assignments to each class. Every teacher accepts his completed assignments, except Florence Kreiger.

She bases his failing grade in her math class on his lengthy unexcused absences.

A failing grade in this advanced math class would keep Jim from qualifying for the School of Mines.

Mother breaks her rule of noninvolvement and makes an appointment with Mr. Haskins, the high school principal.

Miss Kreiger, having been overruled by Mother and Mr. Haskins, barely conceals her rage but gives Jim his usual A anyway.

~ ~ ~

Grandfather and Grandmother have come for a visit. Grandmother and I enjoy sharing a book together when I go to bed. One of Auntie Edna's Book of the Month Club selections, a book of poems by Edgar Alan Poe, arrives during their visit.

When Grandmother reads the poems to me, she laughs until she has to wipe away her tears. She thinks Poe wrote the silliest poetry she ever read.

Poe's poetry must be pretty bad because we have a book of poems written and published by Grandfather's Uncle Davie and up until now, she thought these poems were the silliest poems she ever read.

We feel sad, the house feels empty, and supper doesn't taste as good after Grandmother and Grandfather go back to Canada.

~ ~ ~

The sheriff finds Jim using his squirt gun to squirt water on the backsides of ladies walking past him on Main Street. *Don't try it again or I'll have to tell your aunt,* he warns as Jim surrenders the offending toy.

~ ~ ~

Grandfather and Grandmother have leased the farm and moved to Carman. They bought a house next to the Harris family.

Mr. Harris owns the only haberdashery in town.

Mrs. Harris, deafer than Grandmother, invites me to have tea with her in the afternoon. The Harris' have three daughters but I don't see them often. They have their own friends and I am only in town for a few weeks of summer.

I spend the whole summer with Grandmother and Grandfather. He seems to be gone a lot, just like when we all lived on the farm. When I ask where he goes, Grandmother says to judge cattle at the various fairs in Manitoba, Saskatchewan and Alberta.

If there are none of those damned Shorthorn cattle in heaven, your grandfather will not be happy, she tells me.

Jim spends some time in Carman too. He dates Isabel Stobart, the town beauty.

When Grandfather isn't around, Jim teases Grandmother by grabbing the bottom of her corset, tipping her up on her toes. She shrieks and tries to swat him. The game ends when they both dissolve into tears of helpless laughter.

Barbara spends a little time in Carman too.

Donny Doyle comes to call. They used to play together when they were little. She is a lot taller than he is now.

~ ~ ~

August 20, 1942. The town of Carman sits with its collective ear pressed to the radio. News of the Dieppe Raid is being broadcast. The Saskatchewan regiment of the Queen's Own Cameron has made a daring amphibious landing on the French beach at Dieppe. The broadcast reports that the casualties from the nine-hour battle are heavy.

After the next of kin have been notified, the Winnipeg Free Press prints the first casualty lists. The special edition is ominously large.

Grandmother and Grandfather take the paper into the front room. When Grandfather finishes reading, he takes me to the post office with him. He buys war bonds. The routine of the second day is a repeat of the first. We return from the post office on the third day to find Grandmother still seated on the davenport, the list of casualties on the floor beside her. She looks up, dismayed that we have discovered her in tears.

Next time I walk to the theater to check on what movie is being shown, I stop to read the huge new poster on display. It portrays the regimental piper, in full dress uniform, piping the regiment into battle amid a hail of German bullets. The piper's extraordinary example of valor succeeds. The regiment unwaveringly follows him. The poster declares the raid to be a success.

~ ~ ~

Grandfather answers the doorbell's ring to greet a beaming neighbor who presents him with a bottle of newly made dandelion wine. The wine, poster paint yellow, is in an old medicine bottle stopped with a real cork. Grandfather thanks the neighbor graciously, closes the door, hands the bottle to Grandma, who pours its contents down the kitchen sink.

I wonder what color the wine would have turned the grass.

~ ~ ~

About two blocks up the street from Grandfather and Grandmother's house sits a raggedy old house that sags and tilts awkwardly to the north. All the paint has peeled from its exterior. The gate tightly shut, encloses and equally unkempt yard. In the middle of the front door, a large bright crimson sign warns: **Quarantine**. Grandmother explains that a family of half-breed Indians lives there. Someone in the family has tuberculosis and they are not allowed to leave the property until no one has tuberculosis anymore.

~ ~ ~

Grandma Bruce lives six blocks away from Grandmother and Grandfather Davidson's house in Carman. I have been summoned to make an appearance at Grandma Bruce's. Uncle Bob, home on leave for a few hours decides he wants to meet me.

Grandmother Davidson demands that I rebraid my hair, put on my best dress, polish my shoes before I go.

I remember the directions to Grandma Bruce's house.

I discover how little time it takes to walk six blocks.

Grandma Bruce answers my knock and ushers me into the parlor where Uncle Bob stands, tall and handsome, in his Royal Canadian Air Force uniform. He is a general, Grandma Bruce proudly tells me.

I am asked to sit down while Grandma Bruce and Uncle Bob discuss me in tones low enough that I can't hear the conversation. After a few minutes I am dismissed, allowed to return to Grandmother Davidson's house.

This visit provides the only time I will ever see my father's younger brother. This visit provides the only time I will spend with Grandma Bruce during my last summer in Canada.

~ ~ ~

Grandmother has Grandfather drive us into Winnipeg so that we can go shopping. I am developing breasts she says and I need a brassière. We go to the third story of this large department store where rows and rows of bras sit neatly displayed on large display tables. I ask if we could find a dressing room. Grandmother looks confused. *Whatever for?* she asks. We put various sizes up to my chest. Grandmother selects two garments, the clerk rings them up and puts them in a sack that proclaims *Eaton's* in large print. *You will have to wash these often,* she instructs.

~ ~ ~

Grandmother has asked Dr. Jamieson to the house. He arrives shortly. They go upstairs, into Grandmother's bedroom and close the door. After a while the doctor comes out, his little black bag firmly gripped in his hand. He pats me on the head.

Next evening, Grandmother asks me to get her will. *She is going to die,* I reason. In desperation, I write a letter home. I wait until dark to mail it under cover of darkness. I dare not get caught telling on Grandmother.

The telephone is used exclusively for emergencies.

Before long, Mother arrives in Carman. We go back to the States a few days later.

~ ~ ~

Edna hates the Fourth of July. She spends the day in surgery with various doctors bandaging burns, patching up torn fingers, injured eyes, and displaced noses.

She comes home late in a foul mood.

I wish they'd outlaw those damned firecrackers, she says, and goes to bed.

We bring her many cheese sandwiches with extra butter and salt before she can calm down enough to sleep.

~ ~ ~

I come in from play, filled with misery and tears. Mother tries to comfort me. Between sobs I tell her I have started my period.

How wonderful, she exclaims, *you're a real woman now.*

It is not wonderful! I contradict her. *Now everyone will know why I can't go swimming.*

She sighs, goes into her room, comes out with a sanitary belt and napkin, and leads me into the bathroom for my initiation into womanhood.

~ ~ ~

My menstrual cycle turns into a nightmare of pain. Mother takes me to see Dr. Dawley. Female hormones are a new therapy. These shots contribute to the pain, prolongs the flow and I develop a hand tremor. I tell Edna maybe she needs the shots. I certainly don't. I refuse to keep my next appointment.

~ ~ ~

One of Barbara's Saturday chores requires her to wash my hair. I have long thick hair that she keeps in braids in a vain attempt to keep me looking tidy.

After Barbara sees *For Whom the Bell Tolls,* she takes me to a beauty shop and gives a beauty operator fifty cents to cut my hair exactly like Ingrid's.

I leave the shop with hair two inches in length all over my head. Mother comes home from work that night. She cries and Barbara never has to be responsible for my hair again.

~ ~ ~

During a friendly game of basketball in PE, an opposing player trips me to prevent the unlikely chance of my scoring a basket. My right foot and ankle swell into a massive bruise.

I complain to Auntie Edna. *You are always doing something,* she sighs.

It is the same leg Dr. Jackson set when I broke it the previous winter.

He examines my newly injured leg a few days later. He says it looks like a bad sprain to him.

Three years and two unsuccessful surgical attempts later, attempts to reattach the *post tibialis* tendon, I still limp, still complain of pain, my ankle and foot still swell and bruise.

Mother takes me to see an orthopedic specialist in Sioux Falls. *Go barefoot,* he says, ignoring the ice and snow outside his office window. *You'll be in a brace before you're thirty.*

~ ~ ~

The War Department builds a strategic air base on the prairie a few miles east of Rapid City. Sidewalks on Saint Joe and Main Street seem to be filled with khaki clad men.

Mother says just to walk quickly and look straight ahead and no one will bother me.

At the dinner table, I ask Auntie Edna what a rubber is.

It is a sheath a man puts over his penis so he will not get a woman pregnant during sexual intercourse, is her answer. She is curious why I want to know.

Well, one of the new girls in school was talking about her date from the air base last night and she said his rubber broke and she hoped she wasn't in trouble, I tell her.

I see, Auntie Edna says.

We continue eating dinner.

~~~

I confront Auntie Edna angrily. *Mother is going to be sick again! Just look at the mess in the house. And she never sleeps.*

Edna denies it.

Look at her, I yell. *Can't you see the change in her! Jesus Christ Edna, put her in the hospital before she tries to kill herself again.*

I've talked to your mother. She has promised to be good, Auntie replies through tight lips.

Goddamnitalltohell, Edna, one day I'll be twenty-one and I'll put her in the hospital myself, I shout at Auntie's retreating back. Dick Hart and I hire on at the Custer State Game Lodge for the summer season of 1943. The war makes qualified help scarce.

Dick's job is assistant horse wrangler.

After I complete my chores as the one and only chambermaid, I head for the kitchen. I will spend the rest of the day peeling potatoes in a machine just like the one in Auntie Edna's hospital basement. I make pies for the restaurant. Mother, hired on as cook, shows me how to prepare elk for roasting. I think the job is too hard for her because about half way through the summer, Auntie Edna comes and takes her away. Then I just help in the kitchen but the new cook doesn't spend any time showing me anything.

Horseback riding in the afternoon makes my job tolerable.

Raymond, the head wrangler, ranches in the off-season. He stocks his ranch with cattle he and his common law wife, Frances, rustle from other ranchers.

Raymond says Frances can cut a calf out of a herd better than any man.

A guest has his Tennessee walking horse, Dixie Queen, shipped in and stabled at the Lodge. He never rides the mare, because his belly is so big that he probably can't fit in a saddle, I reason.

He just exercises her on a lead rope every day.

One night after supper, Dick and I smoke a well-deserved cigarette. Dick wonders if I would like to ride the Dixie Queen.

Under cover of darkness, we sneak into the stable. Dick saddles the horse. He lets me ride first. Reluctantly, I return her to Dick. When he finishes his ride, we rub her down and carefully put the tack away.

No one must ever know about our stolen ride.

Horse thievery remains a more serious crime than stealing a car in South Dakota.

~ ~ ~

Mr. Gideon manages the Game Lodge. A short dapper man, he carries a small revolver in a shoulder holster at all times.

I learn of his accuracy with this ever-present hidden weapon when he shoots a squirrel in the eye high up on a tree branch that encroaches on the Annex roof.

He assures me that his action prevents the varmint from causing further damage to the roof.

Mr. Gideon constantly reminds his wife, a stroke victim, *Pull your bloomers up, for God's Sake, Emmy.*

He has a mistress in town.

At the end of an entire summer's ten to twelve hour days, he pays me sixty dollars. When I protest, he reminds me that I also received room and board.

There are no child labor laws in South Dakota.

~ ~ ~

Mother and Clara, Dick's mother, are best friends. Mother thinks I should date Dick because he is such a nice boy. I try to explain to her that the only thing Dick and I have in common is that we both like horses. Besides that, I tell her, he can't even drink one beer without getting goofy.

Years later, after a night of hard, solo drinking; Dick blows his brains out with a cleverly rigged shotgun blast. The only message he leaves his fiancée and his mother is a small note stating that he knew what he was doing.

The Lutheran church refuses to bury him.

~ ~ ~

On the Fourth of July, Mother's favorite holiday, the phone rings. Calling from a dude ranch in Wyoming, Mother wants us to know she is having a wonderful time but has no time to chat.

She is having another psychotic episode, and no one has known where she is or where she has been for two or three weeks. I do not convey the message to anyone. She will be home, sick and broke, before Auntie Edna could find the time to retrieve her.

~ ~ ~

Mother has a job, but it doesn't pay enough to afford dental care. She strikes a bargain with Dr. Johnson. He agrees to fix our teeth. In return, Mother will keep the doctor's books after her regular working hours. Jim returns from his appointment with Dr. Johnson bragging that he needed no Novocain. Barbara experiences equal ease with her dental work, although she did need some Novocain for a really bad tooth.

I am the last to pay this gentle, patient man a visit. He leads me to the dental chair, lowers it, and suggests I climb up and sit down.

I climb up onto the seat and remain standing. *Would you like to sit down?* he asks.

No, I reply.

Will you open your mouth? he asks, stepping far away from the chair.

I deliberate.

He waits.

He is a great bear of a man, all brown of eyes and hair and skin.

I open my mouth.

He never again asks me to sit down. He fixes all my teeth, administering copious amounts of Novocain, while I remain standing on the chair.

～～～

The First Congregational Church of Rapid City sits squarely in the middle of the seven hundred block of Kansas City Street. Sturdily constructed of brown brick, capped with a decorative ledge of limestone, it lacks a steeple. Two stories high, the sparsely decorated exterior indicates its solid connection to the founders of the Plymouth Rock Colony.

The interior contains rows of plain wooden pews. There being no center aisle promotes a communal sense of equality. The stained glass windows, subdued in color, devoid of intricate design, provide decoration for the worshippers.

A great pipe organ compliments the well-rehearsed choir.

Kay Dawley sings soaring solos in her rich contralto voice. Her husband, too busy with his demanding medical practice, rarely enjoys her Sunday offertories.

The Robins, he a local lumber baron and his elegantly groomed wife, attend the church along with the other prosperous townsfolk who have managed to escape the wrath of the Depression.

We attend because Auntie Edna has chosen this particular place for her own personal, political and spiritual reasons.

The minister, Mac Macall, preaches sermons commensurate with the class and moral values of his prosperous flock.

On Mother's Day we accompany Mother to church where we pin the appropriate red carnation to our lapels to indicate that our mother still lives. The white carnations are reserved for those who have dead mothers.

Mr. Macall's sermon focuses on the evils of mothers who work versus the virtues of mothers who stay home. At the end of the service, the Reverend stands at the doorway to greet his parishioners, receive their compliments on his scripturally correct sermon. His fiery red hair gleams in the May sunshine.

As we leave, Mother takes his hand. *Mr. Macall,* she says, *were you speaking directly to me in your sermon, or were you addressing working women in general?*

We quickly gather around Mother, shield her from the fury of the Reverend's glare, escort her down the steps, and treat her to luncheon at the Virginia Café, the best restaurant in Rapid City.

~ ~ ~

After school, while waiting at the hospital for Auntie Edna to take us home, Jim complains of feeling sick. Edna sends him to the lab housed in the basement of the new part of the hospital. Sam Crab, the lab technician, draws some blood, sends Jim back with a report of an elevated white cell count.

Eventually, we drive home, and Jim goes to bed. We eat dinner.

Before daylight, Jim crawls into Auntie's bedroom. He finally rouses the entire household by bellowing, *Goddamn it, Edna, get the hell out of bed. I'm dying, for Christ sake.*

Because he is too ill to help her on with her corset, Auntie Edna takes a long time to dress.

We arrive at the hospital as the sky changes out of grey and into a pale rose.

Jim is admitted to the hospital and prepped for emergency appendectomy surgery.

Barbara crosses the street to eat breakfast with her friend, Alice.

I wait in the lobby of the hospital for school to start.

After school, I search the hospital until I find Jim tucked away on a sun porch. He is out of bed, walking around.

I don't think you're supposed to be doing that, I tell him.

Get the hell out of here, he hisses through clenched teeth.

I return to the lobby, wait for Edna to finish her day's work. Then, with Mrs. Straub sucking her teeth, we drive back to the house at Canyon Lake.

~ ~ ~

Living at Canyon Lake is practically living in the country.

~ ~ ~

Mother, once more high as a kite, decides to raise chickens. Jim and I will care for the little flock after school, thus providing the family with a cheap source of meat, she informs us.

Barbara escapes the assignment because she has an afternoon job in town working in a music store.

Somehow Mother procures a shed sufficient to house a few chickens. We help her place the shed in a little wooded area across the road from our house.

Jim keeps the chickens watered, fed and clean.

On a Friday evening, Mother decides the time has come to slaughter the chickens.

Jim's job is to kill them. I am to help him dress them.

Mrs. Straub's job is to supply the ax.

Mother expects all the chickens to be slaughtered and dressed before she gets home from work on Saturday afternoon.

Saturday morning dawns dark and cold.

Heavy wet snow falls in clumps.

Jim goes next door for Mrs. Straub's ax, which she has set out by her front door.

I follow him.

He picks up the ax and examines it. Holy shit, he mutters, look at this ax, for Christ's sake.

I inspect the ax. The blade is scalloped.

How in the hell am I supposed to kill anything with that? he mumbles, stomping in the direction of the chicken coop.

I follow.

By now we are up to our ankles in light, wet snow.

Don't stand there, he orders. *Get two chickens out of the coop.*

The chickens are slow to respond in the darkness of the snowy day.

I grab two. They protest loudly.

He takes the chickens by the feet, then ties their feet together with a little twine. He then hands the subdued chickens back to me.

An old stump stands close by.

Put the head on the stump! He sighs.

Tears blur my vision.

Hold the goddamn chicken still, he demands.

I turn my head away.

Thump, goes the ax. *Squawk*, screams the chicken.

Jesus Christ, hold the chicken still! he screeches.

I struggle to obey, tears and snotty nose complicating my efforts.

Thump, thump, goes the ax. The chicken's shrieks pierce the snowy quiet of the woods. Jim whispers something sinister.

The chicken ceases to protest.

He grabs the other chicken from my hand, unties its bonds and throws it back into the chicken coop, slams the door shut, picks up the chicken whose neck he has just wrung, hands it to me.

We return to the house with the one dead chicken. We change our bloody, cold, wet clothes.

Mother comes home to one dressed chicken.

The next week, chickens, chicken feed, and coop are gone.

And so is Mother.

～～～

A few days after we get the house put back in order: all the clothes back in the proper closets and proper dresser drawers; pots, pans, spice rack, dishes, and other required kitchen things returned to their proper kitchen places, Edna has us all sit down at the dining room table.

She puts several pills on the table. Some pills are in nicely colored gelatin capsules. Some look a lot like the pills Dr. Jamieson left for me when I had rheumatic fever.

These are the kinds of pills your Mother takes. The colored ones are barbiturates. The white ones are opiates. Next time your mother has an accident and takes too many, I want you to hunt around and find where she keeps her pills. Then I want you to call the hospital and tell them what she took. It helps the staff to know because they can treat her more easily and quickly. .

We carefully open the gelatin capsules, wet our index finger and then taste the white powder. Each capsule has a strange bitter flavor. My tongue feels numb where I touch the white powder to it.

That is what barbiturates taste like, Auntie informs us.

Then we stick out our tongue and lick each plain, hard, white, tablet. They too make my tongue numb. Their flavor is different from the barbiturates.

This is what opiates taste like, Auntie informs us.

Always remember to hunt for her pills. Always remember what they taste like. Auntie informs us.

None of us ever discover her illicit stash.

I remember the difference in the taste of those pills to this day.

～～～

Mattie is the town abortionist. Her occupation is a well-guarded, open secret. As a trained nurse, she understands anatomy, sterile procedure, and surgical techniques. Mattie knows several doctors she can call in an emergency.

Some of the girls who can't afford Mattie end up in Auntie Edna's hospital where they die under the watchful eye of the sheriff.

～～～

Jim joins the Royal Canadian Navy. That he has never seen an ocean is not a deterrent to his enlistment. He joins the navy because he doesn't want to walk to Berlin, he says.

Because I know the alphabet, I have been assigned to telegraphy school, he reports in a letter home.

Upon completing training, he joins the crew of a small American lend-lease corvette. Out of a complement of one hundred and sixty four men, the only sailor to have seen the ocean is the captain. The ship sets sail from Halifax. On the second day out, the ship returns to port. The crew is too seasick to sail any farther.

Jim will spend several months escorting ships from the East Coast to England via the North Atlantic, an enemy as ferocious as the German submarines his ship chases. Jim's experiences aren't all bad he informs us when he comes home on leave. He is given an issue of grog twice a day. The ship docks in Londonderry, Edinburgh, Gibraltar, North Africa, and Marseilles.

~ ~ ~

Barbara doesn't much care for high school, although she enjoys its social aspects. She is waiting until she gets into nurses' training where studying will be important, she tells Edna.

After high school graduation, Barbara joins the Cadet Nurses Corps, a wartime program sponsored by the government to help ease the shortage of trained nurses.

She and her best friend, Marianne, take the train to Tacoma, Washington, where they have been accepted into a nursing school.

~ ~ ~

With gas rationed and most of the nurses and doctors in the armed services, Edna decides we should move back to town, closer to the hospital.

Even though she is entitled to gas ration stamps, Edna sells the car.

We move into a small apartment in a house on Columbus Street.

I hate Jim and Barbara for leaving me alone. I hate the move back to town, the loss of freedom.

Edna is usually at the hospital.

Mother and her friend, Ellen, get drunk a lot, even though they never drink whiskey.

School becomes a safe escape rather than a place to avoid.

~~~

Dr. Fox admits Mother to Edna's hospital because she is suffering from another of her deep depressions.

He treats her with a new anesthesia designed to help soldiers suffering from battle fatigue. He hopes to help her find the cause of her depression.

The experiment fails.

Dr. Fox calls me to the hospital for a consultation. He asks me what I think the best thing would be to do for Mother. Together we decide to place her in the hospital at Yankton where she will not be able to harm herself.

~~~

Now that you're in the ninth grade, I expect As and Bs, Edna demands in a rare appearance at supper. I am dumbfounded that she knows what grade I am in.

As and Bs, she says, *or you can expect to attend school at All Saints.* I know Auntie is not making an idle threat just by her tone of voice.

All Saints, the Episcopalian girl's school in Sioux Falls, insists that the girls wear hats and gloves; go to church every Sunday, study etiquette as well as Latin and algebra. And no one dares to smoke cigarettes.

~~~

As a high school freshman, I experience a renaissance of learning. The wasteland of seventh and eighth grade is forgotten. Selma Song's Latin class opens the door to the mysteries of grammar. Argicola, agricolae, farmer, noun! Categorizing words makes sense at last.

Grasping grammar is the only real benefit I derive from two years of Miss Song's attempted instruction of the classics. I struggle with the written complexities expected of a second-year Latin student. I call Ulysses "Useless" and cut Latin root words from the Rapid City Daily Journal for extra credit.

Not until Juliet Schumacher sits next to me in study hall do I feel secure about obtaining a passing grade while slogging through Caesar's campaigns.

Juliet is not a good Latin student either although she is the most beautiful girl in the twelfth grade.

She has a Caesar pony and shares the forbidden translation with me.

~ ~ ~

Grandmother and Grandfather sell their house in Carman and move to Rapid City. They buy a house on Ninth Street with room enough for all of us. The little red wagon disappears.

~ ~ ~

Mother and Grandmother, seated in the dining room and engrossed in conversation, seem unaware that I have come into the house.

He's contesting the divorce, and the lawyer needs more money, Mother informs Grandmother. *The increased costs will depend on the demands of the Canadian court.* Grandmother sighs.

I slip down the stairs, into the basement, before they can accuse me of eavesdropping.

~ ~ ~

Ten girls form a loose confederation, known as the Gang. We have been in school together, some since junior high, some since Miss Stordahl force-marched us through the fifth grade.

The threads that follow us through our high school career are slumber parties, where the cute boys are, shared homework, slumber parties, fashions, who the cute boys are, church activities, Girl Scouts, Job's Daughters, where the parties are that the boys will attend, what song is at the top of the Hit Parade, who is going steady with whom, slumber parties, who has a date for the Saturday night dance, who is going stag.

I don't care if I have a date for Saturday night or if I go with other girls who don't have a date, just so long as I go dancing.

~ ~ ~

Once, Polly's dad lets the ten of us use his hunting cabin housed in the mountains. Despite our carefully planned menus, we run out of food. I saddle the old horse stabled at the cabin and head out the four miles for more groceries. About half way to Nemo, the horse gets so gimpy that I dismount and we walk the gravel road the rest of the way.

Meanwhile, someone catches, kills and cleans the biggest of the chickens and is stewing it in a pot when I return, hours later, after walking the horse and the supplies back to the cabin.

The chicken turns out to be not only inedible but Mr. Grosz's prize rooster.

It snows; a bobcat leaves its footprints on the porch.

Mr. Grosz is never able to use his horse again for hunting.

~ ~ ~

Within the confines of this safe group, we experiment with alcohol, dye Joanne's blonde hair an outrageous pink, discuss the dangers of sex, become proficient in the use of tobacco, plan parties, and ease each other through the perils and pains of adolescence.

In the summer of 1944, Ken and Lucille, owners and operators of the Chuck Wagon, hire me as a waitress. They don't seem to mind that I am fourteen years old and have never waited tables before.

Noted for excellent steaks, fried chicken, fresh pies, and reasonable prices, the little restaurant enjoys a robust clientele. Situated on the edge of Baken Park, the restaurant fills to overflowing with summer tourists.

I work the split shift, open at six, off at two, back at four, close at ten. I make the most in tips this way. Ken and Lucille pay me twelve dollars per week in cash, freeing me from the need to apply for a social security number.

I become financially independent, able to buy the clothes of my choice, shoes I like.

I buy a pair of sapphire earrings and Dr. Jackson pierces my ears. Because my hair is long, no one discovers my mutilation long past the time needed for healing.

One of my first customers at the Chuck Wagon is hugely pregnant. She has slipped in quietly for a piece of Della's famed homemade pie and a cup of coffee. When I serve her coffee, I spill the cream down the front of her enormous belly. She mops at the cream with her napkin, continues blissfully eating her pie, leaves a large tip.

A young couple, staying at Bacon Park and obviously on their honeymoon, asks if they could have a drink. I bring them the usual glasses of water. He asks if South Dakota is a dry state. *No sir, I* reassures him, *it rains here all the time.*

A regular customer complains that she has found a worm in her vegetable soup. Shocked, I offer to bring her a fresh bowl right away.

A table full of hungry, impatient men demand to be fed immediately. Before I can serve them, one man asks what I would do if he bit my arm. *Bite you right back,* is my snappy reply. They consume huge amounts of food, demand extra service, leave no tip.

Martha, another waitress, tells me Lucille is related to the Barons. *They're Jews, you know,* she informs me.

I have never met a Jew, only read about them in the Bible.

I ask Edna if the Barons really are Jews. The next question I ask is, *How can you tell?*

After school starts, I just work the dinner shift at the Chuck Wagon until it closes for the winter

~ ~ ~

As a worldly sophomore, I no longer conceal my affection for tobacco.

Marlene Dietrich smokes. Marlene is beautiful. Marlene lives a glamorous life.

Perhaps tobacco consumption will work for me even if Jim says I look two and a half ax handles wide and Grandfather tells me I will never be hanged for my beauty.

~ ~ ~

I am struck with, seized by, raging hormones. In spite of the long work hours in summer, the heavy academic load in winter, school and church activities, hormones engulf me, demand my attention.

I enjoy a boy's kissing, hard body, tight embraces, their exploratory hands.

Two ghosts haunt me.

Stronger than the apparition of my grandmother and her Baptist-flavored teachings of Christian purity, lurk the ghosts of venereal disease in Auntie Edna's public health book.

~ ~ ~

The costume necessary to be a bobbysoxer consists of scruffy saddle shoes, white ankle socks, long hair, and a loose fitting Sloppy Joe sweater. A box-pleated skirt completes the ensemble.

I always buy my sweaters at Barons because Mrs. Barons takes my fifty cent down payment, keeps a careful record of my fifty cent payments until I have met the total cost of the sweater, a whopping eight dollars.

~ ~ ~

Grandmother has inoperable cancer, the doctors tell Auntie Edna. She manages an emergency leave for Jim through the International Red Cross.

I am allowed to see Grandmother from the doorway of her hospital room.

Jim sits by her bed, holds her hand.

Barbara remains in nursing school in Tacoma.

Grandmother, home from the hospital calls me into her bedroom. She asks me to read Psalm 103, a promise of God's final healing. When I finish, I kiss her. She holds my hand. *I'm ready to go home,* she says and closing her eyes, dismisses me.

Edna comes from Grandmother's sick room into the dining room. *She's gone,* Edna says. No one moves. Grandfather clears his throat. Eventually he leaves. Jim breaks the silence by stating that he has no one who loves him now.

When the *Rapid City Daily Journal* prints Grandmother's obituary, cancer as the cause of death has never been acknowledged publicly before.

Reverend Macall intones Proverbs 31: *Who can find a virtuous woman? For her price is far beyond rubies,* at Grandmother's funeral.

At graveside, Mother shows a regrettable display of emotion by leaning on Grandfather when the coffin is lowered into its grave,

No one remembers to write or call Barbara to tell her Grandmother has died.

~ ~ ~

Mother has been misbehaving. She has made all sorts of inappropriate and expensive purchases. Sometimes she doesn't come home at night. Sometimes her speech is slurred at the dinner table.

Grandfather decides to take her to the Menninger Clinic. They travel safely to Kansas by train.

They arrive at the clinic where Grandfather stays until she is officially admitted, then takes the train back to Rapid City.

Somehow, Mother gets home before Grandfather does.

So much for the Brothers Menninger, Edna sniffs.

~~~

When discharged from the navy, Jim comes home with several medals, sleep disturbances, and a lifelong affection for grog unlike substances.

After Edna contacts Senator Karl Mundt, Jim receives his benefits from the Canadian GI Bill. He then begins attending classes at the South Dakota State School of Mines and Technology.

~~~

Grandfather has his little black expense account book out.

I'm going to charge you rent, he says.

I sleep in the basement, in the upper bunk bed.

Jim, newly home from the service, sleeps in the lower bunk.

Every night he awakens me with screams, exotic oaths, grinding teeth.

Every night I climb down from the top bunk to waken him from his sweaty nightmares.

You couldn't get a drunk Indian to pay rent for my bed, I tell Grandfather.

~~~

Jim teaches me how to starch and iron shirts. The collar must not be so stiff that it irritates his neck, stiff enough so that it will stay crisp the entire working day. Shirts incorrectly starched and ironed are tossed into the soiled clothes to be rewashed and ironed to acceptable perfection.

He also teaches me how to clean my newly pierced ears and how to shave my legs without dripping blood on everything.

~ ~ ~

Joining Job's Daughters is a big deal. Membership requires both a formal invitation and a male relative who is a Freemason in good standing. Somehow I meet the criteria.

After the initiation ceremony, I notice a picture of a beautiful Minnie and a handsome Charlie Caton prominently displayed in one of the common rooms in the Masonic Temple. Polly digs an elbow into my ribs before I can open my mouth to say something about their now altered social status.

There are many advantages to being a Job's Daughter. First of all, it is a secret organization and no one is supposed to know what we are doing, not even our parents unless they help with the bookkeeping, serve on the advisory committee, contribute to our fundraising talent shows, play the piano to accompany Joanne's solo, or serve as chaperone at one of our many soirees.

But best of all, the DeMolay's help sponsor our formal Christmas dance which is always the best winter party in town.

Working my way up through the ranks of elected offices, I attain the exalted office of Honored Queen. During my reign, we discover that the stuffed dove, a symbol of the purity of the Job's Daughters, has become infested with bugs. Replacing this essential prop puts a serious strain on the treasury.

During her part in an initiation ritual, Lolita, as flighty and beautiful as her unstable mother, misspeaks her lines that inform the initiates of Job's repentance in dust and ashes, and instead announces to the startled assemblage that Job repented in dust and asses.

After some of us leave for college, Lolita's father drives her to Yankton to visit her mother. He obtains permission from his wife's psychiatrist to take her to luncheon in town. On the way back to the hospital he stops the car, shoots Lolita and her mother to death before he turns the gun on himself.

Twila, of Veronica Lake sophistication, suffers a collapse of her garter belt during the recessional march. She strides right along, garters and belt flapping around her feet, keeping time to the solemn march.

As Honored Queen, one of my duties is to take my officers to church, there to be introduced by the minister and applauded by the congregation. The Sunday we attend the First Congregational Church, Reverend Macall introduces neither me nor my officers. Nor does he shake my hand when we leave the service, perhaps as payment for Mother's earlier irreverence.

~ ~ ~

Being Roman Catholic, Audrey, Betty R., Betty F. and Marjorie are unable to join Job's Daughters.

Why would we feel bad? We're invited to all the parties and dances and we don't have to go to any of those dumb meetings, is Audrey's reassuring answer to Mary Katherine's anxious reaction to her first experience with exclusivity.

~ ~ ~

Mother and Edna are gone, leaving Grandfather, Jim and me to fend for ourselves. The Chuck Wagon is closed for the winter; Jim has not yet received his government money for his enrollment in the School of Mines. Grandfather, deciding not to contribute to the delinquency of our leisured life of studies, refuses to buy groceries.

Jim and I search the house for something that can be turned into a meal. We find five pounds of lard, ten pounds of flour, a five-pound bag of raisins and a canister full of sugar, which I turn into raisin pie.

After ten days of raisin pie, even Grandfather needs a respite. He buys some groceries.

It is during the raisin pie famine that I attempt to make baking powder biscuits in hopes of providing variation to our otherwise stultifying diet. Jim eagerly takes a biscuit hot from the oven to the dining room table where he tries to break it open with his fingers. He pries at it with his knife. With great precision, he aims and drops it on an imaginary target on the dining room floor where it sits intact amidst its floury fallout. He eyes the biscuit with resignation, reaches for another piece of raisin pie.

~~~

Rapid City High School, prep school for the South Dakota State School of Mines and Technology, sits between Sixth and Columbus Street. Built of sturdy brown brick with sandstone lintels and terrazzo floors, this large building features up-to-date chemistry and biology labs as well as an outstanding basketball court.

Mr. Prunty prepares the boys for the tough chemistry courses that await them at the Mines.

Girls going to college or nurses training take both chemistry and biology classes.

In chemistry, Mr. Prunty points to the blank spots on a large copy of the Periodic Table of Elements hanging on a classroom wall. Before assigning the task of memorizing the Table, he promises us that someday scientists will discover and name the missing elements.

In Biology, we watch scientific films produced by ERPI Classroom Films. We make the appropriate noises at the beginning of the film when the film producer is announced. After that we maintain rigid silence. There will be a test following the film, and we better know that a lack of potassium caused the goat to go into convulsions.

We memorize Mendel's genetic law, a discovery he made while carefully observing the lowly sweet peas growing in his garden. No one explains why this discovery made by a monk caused such a fuss.

We search diligently for amoebas, bring in many water samples from the creek; capturing one of these elusive creatures would guarantee an A in biology. No one suggests we look in a stagnant puddle of water.

～～～

On a dare, I sit in front of The Hole, a pool hall housed in a basement on the corner of St. Joe and Fifth, a bastion of masculinity where only males enter to play pool and snooker.

There, one afternoon, I beg for alms until Mrs. Dawley walks by.

Does your aunt know what you're doing? Mrs. Dawley demands.

I get up and leave before she can report back to my aunt.

～～～

Miss Olson teaches Euclidian geometry, the only class labeled *math* ever to make sense to me. Following the directions carefully always provides the correct answers. Finding the area of a triangle is sort of like baking a cake; do everything in order, measure properly, success! Charles, the class brain, is called on to recite.

Today, he intones, *I will demonstrate how to circumcise a circle.*

Miss Olson's face remains sweetly calm.

Only respect for her enables us to stifle our laughter.

～～～

Study Hall consumes one hour of every high school day. From her raised dais, Miss Adams keenly observes her students assigned to study tables. She allows nothing but studying.

Doug, a junior who plays varsity football, sits at my table.

He is the first male I find to be more attractive than a horse.

Miss Adams moves him to another table when she discovers that his presence renders me incapable of study.

Study Hall provides a welcome respite from the demands of vigilant excellence expected in the classrooms. I tell Miss Adams I don't feel well. She sends me to the school nurse, who puts me on a cot, covers me with a flannel sheet after I fall asleep. The bell, announcing change of classes, wakens me for my next academic challenge.

~ ~ ~

Grandfather seeks Mother out, finds her in the kitchen ironing. A discussion ensues. The discussion disintegrates into an argument. Grandfather emphasizes his demands by shaking his fist in Mother's face. He turns, opens the door leading to the basement, to begin his descent. Mother unplugs the iron and takes it to the landing. She hurls it in the general direction of Grandfather's head. The iron harmlessly crashes into the basement wall, terminating any further discussion and/or ironing for the day.

~ ~ ~

Katie Moses, tall, bony, gray haired, demands perfection from her sophomore and senior English students. On the first day of my sophomore year, I hand her my admit card. She studies it.

Do you have a brother, Jim? a sister, Barbara? Are you the last Bruce? Sit over there, she sighs, waving me to a seat in the front of the room.

Miss Moses teaches English grammar, how to diagram a sentence, write a paragraph correctly, the importance of a period at the end of each and every sentence, but more important, awards my efforts with an A.

~ ~ ~

Miss Vath teaches creative writing. She always gives me an A for content, F for mechanics. *You can't spell; your punctuation is terrible,* she explains.

~ ~ ~

Mr. Tuttle has been imported from Back East to teach choral music. Anything east of the Missouri is Back East, which makes him a foreigner and somewhat suspect. He is a short, round man with round eyes in a round head. Even his hands are round. He demands more musicianship from his pupils than Mr. Schneider. The lyrics are as important as the notes and he insists that both sounds be produced crisply.

~ ~ ~

After my failures with French horn and cornet, I decide to try out for chorus, despite the fact that Edna says I sing like a cantor in a synagogue.

The top tier in the chorus practice room is reserved for the best singers, progressing down to the worst on the bottom tier. Everyone gets to start out at the top. After just one practice, Mr. Tuttle tells me to sit on the floor.

~ ~ ~

I decide if I wish to make organized sound, I better try out for the Pep Squad.

~ ~ ~

Saturday morning and dressed for work, I decide I should make breakfast for Mother. Once again she is in a deep depression, unable to get out of bed, bathe or eat.

I have to help her to the table. While I am pouring her coffee, she collapses, facedown, into her plate of eggs. I yell for Jim, and the two of us get her back to bed.

We prop her up so that she will not swallow her tongue. She is cyanotic.

While I call Barbara, Jim swabs most of the egg from Mother's face.

Barbara, back from Tacoma and enrolled at St. John's School of Nursing, arrives. I leave for work.

Jim and Barbara will get Mother admitted to Edna's hospital where the sheriff will not bother her.

Attempted suicide is a criminal offense.

~ ~ ~

I have a steady beau. Mother doesn't much like him. Among other things, Don is older than I. When he joins the Marines, she sighs in relief. Absence does not make the heart grow fonder she tells me.

~ ~ ~

Dorrance Dusek becomes a member of the varsity football team. Mrs. Dusek, his mother, becomes the team's biggest fan.

At a snowy game in Lead, Dorrance, handed the ball, exhibits skilled broken field running. Mrs. Dusek paces Dorrance down the sidelines, her broken field running equal to that of Dorrance. The crowd chants Go, Mrs. Dusek! Go! When Dorrance scores the touchdown, Mrs. Dusek is already in the end zone to congratulate him.

~ ~ ~

Mr. Kauffman teaches journalism, a one semester English elective for juniors.

The Pine Needle, the school newspaper, recipient of many awards, provides proof of his effective instruction.

Journalistic writing captivates me.

Mr. Kauffman demands that just the facts, no opinions, appear in the news stories. Opinions belong on the editorial page, Mr. Kauffman informs the class. The fact that the paper prints no editorials goes unnoticed.

To develop my journalistic skills, Mr. Kauffman assigns me the task of interviewing John Sebastian, a harmonica player.

Under contract with the Community Concert Series, Mr. Sebastian will present an evening program of classical music, the high school auditorium his concert hall

Mr. Sebastian agrees to an afternoon interview in the empty auditorium. He arrives promptly for his appointment.

All my careful notes, planned questions, slither from my mind.

Mr. Sebastian, a creature from another world, arranges his long, lanky body on one of the sparse institutional seats. He smiles.

I have never before seen a man with manicured nails, hands unscarred by work. I have never been around a man this smoothly barbered, smelling richly of forbidden thoughts.

He graciously provides answers to my stumbling questions.

Back in journalism class, I am asked how the interview went. *I don't know*, I whisper, struggling to turn my scrambled notes into a newspaper article fit for publication in *The Pine Needle*.

Mr. Kauffman, pleased with the John Sebastian article, asks me to interview Mr. Haskins, the school principal.

Having been interviewed many times before, Mr. Haskins ignores my eager presence, poised pen, open notebook. He dismisses me with a copy of the facts he expects to be included in the story.

I search the paper's morgue for further information.

The article printed in *The Pine Needle* pleases both Mr. Kauffman and Mr. Haskins.

Mr. Kauffman submits my Mr. Haskins interview to the state journalism contest.

At the awards ceremony I receive first prize for best news story, the prize being a membership in the Quill and Scroll Club. The presenter looks at me quizzically, hands me my certificate indicating that the committee, having never met me before and because of the masculine spelling of my name, mistook me for a boy.

~ ~ ~

Mr. Kauffman also teaches a required class called Economics, a subject as mystifying as algebra. Fortunately he seats his students alphabetically. I sit next to Jim Brickley who understands this unfathomable required subject. That I might graduate, he allows me to copy his tests.

~ ~ ~

Coming home from a party, Myrtle asks me if it is true that my mother is crazy. *Certainly not!* I lie. At home, in bed, unable to sleep, I decide I have to get the hell out of this town.

~ ~ ~

After careful study of my reflection in the mirror, I complain to Mother.

It's not fair Mom. Jim is so handsome and Barbara is so good looking. What happened to me?

My porcelain-doll mother chuckles. *Don't worry about it, Marion,* she assures me, *it's all the same in the dark.*

~ ~ ~

My admit card for my senior year mistakenly assigns me to College Algebra, taught by Florence Kreiger.

I head back to the principals office to correct the mistake, but to no avail.

Reluctantly, I arrive at Miss Kreiger's classroom and present the admit card. Seated at her desk Miss Kreiger gives careful scrutiny to my name. She scowls.

Are you Jim Bruce's sister?

My regrettable relationship to Jim earns me a grade so low that I am kept from graduating cum laude. I have met Miss Krieger's need to avenge the humiliation she suffered three years ago when my brother and mother defied her authority.`

~ ~ ~.

All Saints is no longer a threat. When it snows, I stay home, smoke cigarettes, drink coffee, and play cribbage. Besides, I have been matriculated by Yankton College.

~ ~ ~

The war has ended. Exhausted from managing the hospital with few trained nurses and fewer doctors, Edna collapses, stricken with rheumatoid arthritis.

Confined to bed at home, Edna follows the doctor's orders of rest and exercise. The newest treatment for this crippling disease consists of shots of gold salts. I ask her if she dies and we cremate her, will we find little gold flakes in her ashes. She laughs, explains the hoped for curative effect of gold salts and why she will never be a viable source of gold ore.

To exercise, Edna plays endless games of solitaire while seated at the dining room table. When she can sit no longer she has someone help her back to bed.

She leaves for Arizona to spend the winter with a cousin in Tucson, I sleep better not having to listen to her nightly groaning and moaning.

When Edna returns in the spring, she sports a tan.

She now understands why the Indians call us paleface, she says.

She still demands that cheese sandwiches with extra butter and salt be brought to her in bed.

I will never amount to anything when I refuse to stay home to take care of her instead of going to a Saturday night dance, she states.

~ ~ ~

Jim and I chance to meet each other in the kitchen. He grabs my arms, his eyes dark with anger. *If I ever catch you in the Rainbow Room, I'll kill you*, he hisses into my face.

I'll go where I damned well please, I hiss back.

He releases my arms to get a firm grasp of my hair, slams my head into the refrigerator door. *I mean it*, he whispers.

I try to reach his face, kick his shins; he slams my head into the refrigerator door again. I grab the thick black curly hair on his forearms.

Wham, goes my head; rip goes the hair from his arms.

We soon tire of the struggle.

Next time I have a date, I suggest we drop in at the Rainbow Room, the newest bar in town. There, people sit at cocktail tables, engage in quiet conversation, sip their drinks. The main attraction, a spinning mirrored ball, reflects light, throws it on the walls and ceiling. I order a Tom Collins a nice drink for a lady, the waitress informs me. I experience an unladylike reaction to the gin.

To avoid Jim's wrath over my incredible intoxication, my date safely delivers me to Mary Katherine's house, where I recover enough from my near poisoning the night before to go to work the following morning.

I never stop in at the Rainbow Room with its spinning ball again.

I never consume gin again, never.

~ ~ ~

Stan Neil and I have known each other since the fifth grade. Stan's mother died when he was born. Mr. Neil indulges Stan with providing his every wish. Stan takes up flying during our senior year. On a cloudless afternoon in May, he dies in an unsuccessful attempt to land his plane.

~ ~ ~

Morris, the shyest boy in the junior class has invited me to the Junior-Senior Prom. He arrives at the front door at the correct time, with the expected corsage. Before I can answer the doorbell, Jim and his friend, John Hoon open the door. They escort Morris inside. After they take the corsage from Morris, they begin The Inquisition.

What kind of a car does Morris drive? Is there enough gasoline in the tank to get to the dance and back? At what time can they expect me home? Are his intentions honorable or dishonorable? How much did he pay for the corsage?

Morris shows Jim the necessary tickets and the dance program.

I try to intervene.

They check out Morris's suit, tie, and shoes.

Finally, Jim pins the corsage on my dress. *Because, Morris*, he says, *you might accidentally poke her with the corsage pin. Have fun*, he says.

The minute the dance is over, Morris hurriedly drives back to the house, lets me out of the car. He does not escort me back to the door.

In reporting this latest travesty of brotherly love to Mother, I sob loudly all the while maintaining I will have to leave town to find a boy who will marry me.

~ ~ ~

I have been graduated. That none of my family was there to witness my accomplishment disappoints me. A friend and I share a couple of beers. I return home early. Tomorrow demands that I be at the Chuck Wagon, on time, to earn as much money as possible.

~ ~ ~

Officially a college woman now, I eagerly anticipate living in a place where rational thought reigns supreme, away from Mother's frenzied behavior, and Edna's unreasonable demands.

~ ~ ~

Part 4:
The Fledgling 1947–1951

Six of the ten members of the Gang resolve to go to college. Mary Katherine and Polly choose the university at Vermilion. Shirley and Betty pick Concordia in Minnesota. Joanne and I choose Yankton College.

Because Joanne never swears, drinks, or smokes, she is selected to receive the Congregational Church's scholarship to Yankton.

I am awarded a job waiting tables in the dining hall to cover the cost of my food.

~ ~ ~

Situated on the Missouri River bluffs, the town of Yankton enjoys the reputation of a progressive town.

The Sacred Heart compound of hospital, nursing school, convent and chapel dominates the highest bluff.

The State Mental Hospital where Mother takes up residency upon occasion, sits perched on another hill far from the center of town.

Yankton College, celebrated for being the first institution of higher learning in the Dakotas, rests on another bluff. I will reside on this hill for the next three and a half years.

WNAX, the most powerfully broadcast radio station in the United States, proudly hosts Lawrence Welk and his polka band.

Senator Gurney, Gurney Seeds and Catalogue and the Gurney Hotel contribute to the awesomeness of this small town's institutions.

~ ~ ~

Jim takes me to the train depot, where I begin my four hundred mile trip to Yankton.

Before I climb aboard, he shares an important fact about academia with me. You will get a professor who will tell you black is white. Always agree. Remember, he has the grade book.

He kisses my cheek good-bye.

~ ~ ~

Joanne and I arrive on campus having freshly graduated from high school. We are accompanied by our old high school boyfriends, Don and Kelly. Both have recently been discharged from the United States Marines. They have turned into our college freshman beaux. Mother was wrong about absence and the heart.

Joanne is financially secure with her scholarship.

Don and Kelly are financially secure on the GI Bill.

I am secure only in the determination to do something else with my life besides wait tables at the Chuck Wagon.

I arrive on campus, to find I have been assigned to the men's dormitory, something about spelling my name using the masculine form.

Reassignment to Kingsbury Hall, the women's residence, happens immediately.

My roommate does not believe in bathing.

I give her my deodorant. I remind her cleanliness is next to godliness. Nothing motivates her to bathe.

Because women are not allowed to smoke within the confines of Kingsbury Hall, I find no respite from the increasing stench of Laura's unwashed body, unchanged bed linens, moldering heap of unwashed underclothes.

The dorm is filled to capacity. No one wants to trade roommates.

~~~

With my summer earnings, a small savings account, a couple of redeemed war bonds, I manage to pay tuition, dorm fees and student fees. Unable to buy the most expensive texts, I borrow the necessary books from anyone willing to let me use their copy when they are through studying.

Returning veterans on the GI Bill have crowded college campuses across the country to bursting, leaving books in short supply.

This group of men in my freshman class of less than seventy students set new standards for academic excellence. These veterans of World War II have a low tolerance for academic nonsense. One returned veteran, in an attempt to ease the Calvinist austerity from the campus, makes it possible to buy a shot of whiskey from his locker any time classes are being held. Upon discovery, the offending seller is summarily dismissed from this most Christian of institutions.

~~~

Most students eat in the common dining room in Kingsbury Hall where, as waitress, I earn my work-scholarship.

The food served lacks edibility. The veterans complain they ate better on C rations.

An article in the student paper states that man cannot live by bread alone but with the aid of beans. This statement, viewed as outrageous sacrilege, brings forth an angry uproar among the alumni.

~~~

Don asks me if I would like a ride home for Thanksgiving.

I jump at the chance, surprising myself by how much I miss home.

We leave after dinner on Wednesday, arrive in Rapid City the next morning a couple of hours before the sun.

Dropped off at my house, I ring the doorbell several times. Finally Mother warily unlocks the door.

Wanna buy some magazines? I'm working my way through college, I shout.

Stunned by my unexpected appearance, she grabs my shivering body, pulls me into the warm house.

After feasting on real food for three days, I happily return to Yankton.

~ ~ ~

One night, shortly after the Thanksgiving holiday, I have a dream. Mother and I are climbing a long, brilliantly lit, white patent leather staircase. She, stops, turns, and waves me away. Then she continues on her solitary upward sweep. This dream is my passport into adulthood.

~ ~ ~

Joanne manages to attend school for one semester before she drops out, returns to Rapid City with Kelly, marries him in the church after she converts to Roman Catholicism and before her pregnancy becomes terribly obvious.

After Joanne's fall from grace, Reverend Macall and his board of trustees remain unmoved by my ability to remain on the Dean's List. I had hoped my outstanding scholarship would conceal my occasional drinking, consumption of tobacco, colorful vocabulary and the fact that I had been confirmed in the Episcopal Church.

~ ~ ~

At the end of my freshman year, Jim visits the First National Bank of the Black Hills where Mr. Browning, the bank manager, personally accepts Jim's signature as collateral on a small loan for educational purposes. Jim telegraphs the thirty-five dollars to Yankton. I pay my debts, buy a bus ticket with the remaining funds and have five cents left over for a cup of coffee to sustain me on the long trip back home.

Hours and hours later, Jim greets me at the bus depot. *Got any money left,* he asks hopefully.

Mother and Edna are back East visiting relatives.

Grandfather is judging cattle for the Shorthorn Association somewhere in Canada.

Once again Jim and I search the house for sustenance. We find one jar of pears and thirteen packages of lime Jell-O. Jim opens the pears; I boil water, make several packages of Jell-O then combine the two ingredients.

While we are waiting for our dinner to set, Paul arrives at the door.

Buy you a beer, he offers.

After the second beer at the Anchor Bar, I thank Paul for his generosity. Man cannot live by bread alone, but with the aid of beer, I happily inform him.

~~~

Barbara decides to marry; to marry John Hoon. I can't imagine why she wants to marry any of Jim's friends. She has set her wedding date for February 28, when she could have chosen the twenty-ninth as 1947 is a leap year, thus avoiding all those wedding anniversaries. Both John and I think her choice not to be different is a mistake.

The Dean allows me to leave school for a few days to be the maid of honor after I promise to make up the missed assignments.

Barbara meets me at the train. Hello, Edna, she says after noting my alarming increase in girth.

Despite the weather, the ceremony at the First Congregational Church begins on time. Barbara, elegant in white velvet, is given in marriage by Doctor Jackson. Jim, handsomely suited, serves as best man, and I, my bulk encased in blue taffeta, complete the wedding party. The nuptials, borrowed from the Episcopal Book of Common Prayer, and performed by Reverend Macall, celebrates the union witnessed by almost all of the 150 invited guests.

The day before the wedding, John's brother and stepmother, and Paul pick up Don in Yankton. A prairie blizzard forces them to seek shelter in Kimball for the night. The blizzard abates, the De Soto's gas line thaws, and they drive into Rapid City too late for the celebration. They even miss the reception where Reverend Macall informs various guests he expects the union will last no longer than six months.

~ ~ ~

Barbara, now a registered nurse, has a job with an eye surgeon in Lincoln, Nebraska where John is enrolled in the Elgin School of Watchmaking. They honeymoon on their way to Lincoln driving John's gray 1938 Plymouth stuffed with their elegant wedding gifts as well as their mundane worldly goods.

John's brother and stepmother, and Paul drop Don and me off at Yankton on their way back to Lincoln. On a lovely spring evening, Don asks me whether I would like to go with him to the Depot Café.

Because the coffee available in the dining hall is undrinkable and I am too broke to buy coffee, I happily accept his offer.

The Depot Café, an old rattletrap of a building, sits at the bottom of the campus hill located a good six feet from the railroad tracks.

Jack, owner and operator of the café, welcomes college students who linger over his fresh strong coffee, occasionally buy a beer, and sometimes a sandwich. Because of his personality, his little café does a brisk business.

While we are comfortably seated in the back booth enjoying coffee and conversation, another customer enters.

Suddenly, all the customers in the little café stand up, raise their hands in the air, slowly back up to where we are seated.

Don pokes me. *Stand up*, he says.

I move out of the booth to find myself looking into the barrel of a small revolver. As I ease into an upright position, the revolver points in the general direction of my belly.

Jesus, I announce, *I don't even have a nickel to pay for my coffee.* The revolver wavers.

The gunman, glassy-eyed, shaky, slurred of speech, invites everyone to sit down so that Jack can serve us a fresh cup of coffee. His behavior reminds me of Mother, sans gun.

Sitting at the counter, the young delinquent puts his revolver in his pocket after he shows Jack all the bullets in the chamber.

Jack provides the necessary distraction by serving him a cup and a saucer overflowing with coffee while the rest of us leave.

Once outside we rush to the house next to the café, call the police, rush back up the hill to the safety of the campus.

Inside the dorm, I call home. Mother accepts the collect call.

I've just been held up, I tell her.

She seems unmoved by the news. She asks, *How are your grades?*

A few days later, the Yankton newspaper reports the arrest of two brothers who had been driving around the countryside, taking turns terrorizing restaurant and gas station owners by brandishing a loaded revolver or a sawed-off shotgun at them and their customers.

Sons of a prosperous farmer, they were high on drugs, just out having some fun, the paper reports.

~ ~ ~

Rather than see me work at the Chuck Wagon for the summer, Don helps me get hired on at the Reptile Gardens.

Brainchild of a School of Miner, Earl Brockelsby has chosen to house his snake collection in a large building on the main road from Rapid City to Mount Rushmore. He advertises his establishment with Wall

Drug Store-type signs that clearly direct tourists where to stop at his reptilian collection before they reach the fabled mountain.

His collection of prairie rattlesnakes, along with a few other reptiles he has purchased, comprise his meager zoo for which he charges a minimal fee for a guided tour. To view the reptilian exhibits, tourists must first pass through the souvenir shop, meet their guide who safely leads them among the cages of snakes, then exit the exhibit through another door leading back into the shop.

One of the sources of income at the Reptile Gardens comes from the ashtrays assembled in a little factory at the back of the retail store. Using plaster of Paris, two workers turn mineral specimens Earl hauls in from his forays into the Hills into charming ashtrays.

These bona fide souvenirs sell like hot cakes at the price of twenty-five and fifty cents each.

The one-dollar-fringed-satin-souvenir-pillow-covers also enjoy brisk sales.

Black Hills gold is much admired but seldom bought, as it represents a major portion of most vacation budgets.

Work hours at the Reptile Garden begin at 7:00 a.m., end at 7:00 p.m. one week, begin at 7:00 a.m., and end at 9:00 p.m. the next week. At noon, Della serves a wonderful meal to all the employees except Mum, Earl's pet skunk. She enjoys a generous serving of bacon.

Mum, one of a litter of four infant skunks Earl found while hunting for snakes, survived the demusking surgery. Affectionate and cuddly, she provides more fun than any kitten. When frightened, she stamps her feet and throws her tail in the air. To our delight, her disabled defense mechanism scatters the tourists.

I develop a friendship with Frances Red Tomahawk, interpreter for the Sioux in Washington DC, classmate of Jim Thorpeand master of the English language, and a guide through the snake displays housed in The Reptile Garden.

He teaches me how to cure menstrual cramps by sipping some of the Old Crow whiskey he keeps tucked away in the soda pop cooler.

He mourns the fact that his beautiful daughter is only half Indian, tells stories of cattle roundups and stampedes; life on the prairie before barbed wire and too many white men spoiled the land.

During the long work days, I wedge myself between the counters and nap standing up. The old injury to my right foot causes both foot and ankle to swell and bruise as the result of endless hours standing on concrete floors.

But I earn six hundred dollars before summer's end, quit in time to rest up, buy some clothes, and prepare for another year of college.

~ ~ ~

Employment at the Reptile Gardens provides me with several pivotal experiences. At after-hour parties, I learn that Cuba Libras are as good to drink as whiskey.

Once again, Mrs. Barons helps me dress appropriately. She is surprised that I have gone from a size 14 to a size 10 since she helped me select clothes the previous fall. *School and working at the Reptile Gardens must be good for you*, she comments.

~ ~ ~

I decide to contact my father.

I have no conscious memory of my father. His name has never been mentioned in my presence. Mother's wedding picture, carefully cut in half, leaves Dad and anyone to the right of him omitted from the photographic commemoration. Mother is seated, stiffly gowned in bridal white, her veiling secured by a wreath of orange blossoms.

I cannot recall who gave me Dad's address in Calgary. Perhaps it was Edna. Certainly it was not Mother.

From this impoverished memory I write: *Mother and I have managed this far. I need your financial help to continue with my education.*

Dad promptly responds to my letter. He will send me fifty American dollars for every month I spend in school. Based on his letter, I register for another year at Yankton College.

September 1948 I am back in school with my summer earnings and Dad's first bank draft. I am solvent, able to buy books for all my classes this semester.

October's check comes with a request for my course of studies. The Canadian government has an interest in its citizenry's investments, Dad explains. I send him a copy of my first year's grades.

November's check arrives with the news that Dad will be spending Thanksgiving with me. He will come to Yankton by bus the Sunday before the holiday. The two of us will continue on to Lincoln, Nebraska, there to celebrate the day with Barbara and John. When we return to Yankton, Dad will continue on to Rapid City to visit Jim.

I am numbed by the news. It never occurred to me that for one hundred and fifty dollars this man could have purchase on my life. I made no bargain with him to be my father, only that he should contribute to my education.

The Sunday of his arrival dawns cold and overcast. By noon the snow is falling. As the day wears on, my anxiety and the storm increase in intensity. I break the rules and call home, collect.

Edna, I plead, *Dad will be here in a couple of hours and you have to help me! What does he look like?*

Bing Crosby, how are your grades? she replies.

By seven o'clock the snowfall increases in intensity. I trudge down to the bus depot only to find a note on the locked door with the information that due to the blizzard, the bus has been delayed indefinitely. I write the dormitory phone number on the notice along with a note to Dad to call me when he arrives in town. I slog back to the dorm through the increasing fury of the storm, grateful to a universe so ordered that I am spared trying to decide which man getting off the bus looks the most like Bing Crosby.

Dad calls me from the Gurney Hotel Monday morning. I find a substitute to serve my tables, cut classes for the rest of the day and head downtown, through the snow.

When Dad opens his hotel room door, I am struck by how small he is, how blue his eyes are, how he looks nothing like Bing Crosby.

Wednesday we travel to Nebraska, celebrate Thanksgiving on Thursday.

Friday night we go to the Legion Hall to dance, gamble, and see who can consume the most whiskey.

Saturday morning Dad asks me if I have a hangover.

Never on Scotch, I tell him.

Christ Almighty, he says, *you're some kid.*

~~~

I overhear a political discussion in the Student Union. Fascinated, I sit down and listen to the divergent opinions. When the debate ends, still unresolved, I explain to Bob, a returned veteran from New York and a proponent of the New Deal, that I had never met a Democrat before. He said he was proud to be able to expand my horizons.

~~~

The roommate assigned to me during my sophomore year develops into one of life's fortunate accidents. Joyce, a two-year education student, endures me with pragmatic stoicism. She uncomplainingly tidies up after me, never comments on my endless messiness, wakens me early for breakfast duty, and invites me home for weekends.

Her mother Bess, veteran school teacher and accomplished cook, and her father Tape, musician turned auto mechanic who quietly drinks away his dreams, welcome me into their comforting home.

Tape, uncle of Juliet of the Latin Pony, takes us rabbit hunting. Bess makes hasenpfeffer from the rabbits we bring home.

Joyce and I take the leftover feast back to school; devour it in place of the questionable creamed dish of the day available in the dining hall.

~ ~ ~

Jim, having graduated from the Mines, marries. His wedding to Geraldine, a childhood friend, takes place in Winnipeg during the worst flood in the history of the city. I am too busy writing finals to join Mother and Edna for his elegant nuptials.

~ ~ ~

Housing in the women's dorm is a statement of status. A room on the third floor designates the lofty achievement of an upper classman. This perch provides a view of the campus, the river, and a clear shot at Fryborg's nocturnal escapades. Fryborg, son of a wealthy and prominent member of the community, is a flasher, his favorite flashing spot being Kingsbury Hall. Any upperclassman sighting him is duty bound to stick her head out of her room and announce the exact location of Fryborg's presence. The cry of *Fryborg on West Wing* causes a rush to the west wing. Windows are thrown open, whistles and catcalls of appreciation soon turn the quiet campus air into a raucous din. Fryborg wins extra approval during the winter months when it takes an act of bravery just to open the window. Sometimes when we are coming home from Sunday dinner or an evening at the movies, Fryborg will greet us at the top of Observatory Hill, coat and pants wide open. Because it does no good to report him to the police, we decide we might as well enjoy his unusual greeting. We acknowledge his presence by calling out, *Hi Fryborg, nice night.*

~ ~ ~

I am no better at college Spanish than I was with high school Latin. When called on to translate from *Una Noche Oscura en Lima*, I call the main character Peter Gonads. Miss Dunham winces. To help me complete the required two years of foreign language, Miss Dunham, in an uncharacteristic fit of mercy, assigns me a small Spanish novel to read, after which I am to submit a book report written in Spanish.

I spend hours struggling to comprehend the worn, little volume. A student from Argentina seeks me out, offers to write the book report for me for the reasonable sum of five dollars. For the first time in my life, I experience the true meaning of salvation.

~ ~ ~

Mother receives my grades for the third semester. Once again I am on the dean's List. Edna calls long distance to ask why I received a C in Spanish.

It is then that I decide to join in the fun and games of college life.

I prefer the company of men. They laugh at dirty jokes, play Whist instead of Bridge, see who can drink a dime beer by picking up the glass with their teeth without breaking the glass, who can drink the most Fearless Fosdicks (a concoction of two thirds of a shot glass full of whiskey topped off with Peppermint Schnapps), smoke endless cigarettes, get the best grades.

Their company proves a lot more exciting than the girls and their preoccupation with perceived weight loss or gain, clothes, hair styles, Bridge proficiency, correct table settings for the upcoming Dean's Tea or comparative studies of karat weight in diamond engagement rings.

If I wish to go to dances, out to dinner on Sunday night when the dining room is mercifully closed, I need a date, not a buddy. Most girls have a steady fellow. I manage to cultivate a man from back East who thinks my behavior a refreshing change from the Eastern girls he has previously known. He speaks French, has money from home in addition to his GI Bill, and plays football, albeit not exceedingly well.

I am smitten.

Because I mistakenly interpret his ardor as a proposal of marriage, I follow him to the East Coast for summer vacation. I find employment as a waitress in a restaurant on New Jersey's South Shore where I work half the hours I worked at the Chuck Wagon, make twice the tips. At the end of summer, my lover resolutely puts me on the train, kisses me good-bye, then tells me he will not be seeing me, again, ever.

I return to Yankton, resolve to complete my course of study in record time. I have to get the hell out of this school.

~~~

The prerequisites to advanced psychology classes are nine units in philosophy; the theory being that psychology is just another philosophy. I study a vast assortment of learned men's approach to reality. I get lost in the language. It seems silly that Kant takes pages to restate, "Judge not that ye be not judged." *Das Kapital is* beautifully written but the premise proposed by Marx, first recorded in the Acts of the Apostles, seems predestined to failure. Machiavelli sounds too much like Adolph Hitler to be taken seriously. I enjoy the Greeks who seem to have the most intelligible grip on reality with their recorded observations of the vagaries of human behavior.

~~~

In ethics class, the professor suggests that Jesus may have been hallucinating when he met temptation in the desert. *After all*, he asks, *if you had no food or water for forty days, don't you think you would see things?* The theology students rise up en masse, claim blasphemy, and seek the professor's dismissal. The next lecture in class covers the ethics of questioning a belief system to test its validity. The theology students rise up en masse, once again claim blasphemy, seek the professor's dismissal. The next lecture covers the difference between religious thought and scientific inquiry.

~~~

After accepting the gynecologist's opinion that Barbara will never become a mother, she and John opt for the next best thing. They place an order for a brand new car. Two weeks before the automobile's due date, Barbara discovers she is not only capable of but is well into the process of becoming a mother. They cancel the car, continue driving the 1938 Plymouth, and happily accept Bruce upon delivery thus making February 17, 1948 a day to always to be celebrated joyously.

~~~

On a cold bright winter day, the students in the abnormal psychology class and a group of student nurses from Sacred Heart meet in an equally cold bright lecture hall at the State Hospital for the Insane.

Seated at a table on a small stage, a psychiatrist presents inmates suffering from a variety of mental illnesses.

First the psychiatrist lists symptoms of the disease. Then an attendant ushers in a patient to demonstrate the described disease. The psychiatrist's skillful interviewing allows us to take notes outlining the patients' symptoms. We are introduced to patients suffering from schizophrenia, paranoia and many forms of dementia including dementia caused by alcohol abuse.

We are dismissed after the final patient, a manic depressive, demonstrates the result of a frontal lobotomy to help control his mood swings. His zombie like answers during the interview leave me unable to hold a pencil.

After two and one half interminable hours, I endure the ride back to the dorm. Once safely inside, I throw up, remove my sweat soaked clothes, collapse into bed. Mother is in residence at the hospital and I feared the psychiatrist would present her as a classic example of manic depression.

~~~

To dine in Kingsbury Hall requires a spirit of culinary adventure. The faculty table, placed at the head of the large noisy room, permits a separating distance from the student tables.

Mother Page, the housemother of Kingsbury Hall, serves both as host and hostess to members of the faculty unfortunate enough to have no other choice in dining arrangements.

The rest of the tables seat ten students each with the host at the head of the table, at the table's foot, the hostess.

The responsibility of polite and appropriate conversation rests with the table's assigned host and hostess. Mother Page decides who presides over the meals, using a rotation system so that all students experience responsibility for civilized conversations during civilized dining.

When Mother Page serves her version of breaded pork chops, any student finding a piece of meat among his or her portion of breaded pork fat stands, holds the morsel impaled on a fork high overhead and shouts, *I got the prize*, then sits to appreciative applause.

Occasionally a student in physiology class dissects a pregnant cat. The embryos, slipped into a bowl of creamed dish du jour, clears the table as the offending bowl is passed around.

Mother Page unerringly presents her extraordinarily creative dish of creamed noodles the same day Biology 102 presents a lab on tapeworms.

Bits of hard boiled eggs hidden in cream sauce the consistency of wall paper paste give new meaning to meatless Wednesdays and Fridays during Lent.

Only grizzled veterans are able to consume the dark oily concoction foisted off as coffee.

A few boys have wandered up North for their education. During freshman initiation, at a given signal, one rises from his seat at the table and shouts, *save your Confederate Money boys, the South will rise again.* He is seated to thunderous applause.

Few hardy souls present themselves at the dining hall on Saturday morning. As a result I am relieved of breakfast duty every other weekend. Host and hostess are absolved from their social responsibilites.

The bullpen, a room that provides shelter from the elements for men waiting for admittance into the dining hall, houses few.

Attendance at the faculty table is negligible. A handful of dorm residents straggle down into the dining room to consume Mother Page's unusual pancakes, a breakfast dish that lies undigested in the stomach for hours.

On an ordinary wintry Saturday morning, a table far away from the facility table and closest to the bullpen demands an inordinate amount of pancakes. Because no limits exist on how much food can be served, platter after platter of pancakes is delivered to the all-male, no-host table.

Toward the end of the meal the source of the gluttony, a mange infested, scrawny, stray dog wobbles away from the table. This creature from the Black Lagoon staggers up to the faculty table. It leans its head on an empty chair next to Mother Page and throws up all her indigestible pancakes.

Rumors circulate of an administrative decision to expel each and every member of the offending table but none of the waiters or waitresses can remember exactly who was seated there.

I eat at the waiter's table the entire time I attend Yankton College, proving that, given a choice in food selection, academic life can be sustained on a diet of Rice Krispies and diluted milk.

~ ~

My menstrual cycles continue in their ferocity. After I use up all the whiskey that Dr. Jackson carefully bottled with an Rx for menstrual cramps, the dean of women sends me to see Dr. Peterson. He examines me, pats me on the leg after the exam and says I will be fine after I have my first baby. He becomes offended when I ask him to recommend a clean young man for me.

~ ~

Mother, Edna and Grandfather move to Pierre. Both Mother and Edna have accepted jobs with the State Department of Health, Edna as hospital consultant, Mother as secretary to the director of the Department of Health.

Edna calls me just before Christmas vacation.

She is in Mitchell. If I can get from Yankton to Mitchell, she will give me a ride to Pierre and introduce me to a nice young man she works with.

When I arrive in Mitchell, Edna makes me comb my hair and put on some lipstick before she introduces me to Richard, a civil engineer who went to school with Jim and works in the Department of Health. He is tall, slender, exudes testosterone. I am entranced.

Eighteen months later, I am able to convince him he wants me to be the mother of his children.

~~~

When President Truman sends troops to Korea in a police action to keep the world safe from Communism, the reserves are called up.

Newly married and newly graduated from Nebraska University, Paul, Jim's friend who rescued us from pears with Jell-O by buying us beer, and a member of the Air Force reserves, reluctantly leaves for Roswell, New Mexico.

Jim says he volunteered the first time; they'll have to dig him out of the hills if they want him to participate a second time.

On campus, Filthy Bill, a veteran of the European war is called up. He joined the Army Reserves after his discharge, thinking he could use a little extra money while going to school on the GI Bill.

Art, who left a leg somewhere in Europe, says he has an agreement with his draft board to fight every other war.

I am too involved in trying to complete the 120 units necessary to secure a January 1951 graduation to care much about some quarrel in a remote little Asian country that is short of policemen.

~~~

Barbara and John possess two extra tickets to the University of Nebraska homecoming football game, a feat akin to getting front row seats to Broadway's latest smash hit, *Guys and Dolls*.

Richard drives from Aberdeen to Yankton in his spiffy new 1950 Studebaker. We continue on to Lincoln for the game of the year. According to the Cornhuskers, All American Bobby Reynolds is the greatest running back in the history of college football. It must be true because in the closing minutes of the game Bobby is handed the ball, runs, picks up a block, reverses his field, picks up a block, reverses his field, reverses his field again. All in all, he runs over what seems like several lengths of the football field before he scores the winning touchdown. The huge stadium, awash in red shirts, erupts into a frenzy of triumph.

After stopping to celebrate the game at a bar only college students would tolerate, Richard and I return to reality. We drive back to Yankton where I resume grinding out my undergraduate degree. He returns to Aberdeen where he continues grinding out reports on the purity of the water supply east of the Missouri River.

~ ~ ~

College has lost some of its allure. An English literature professor gives me a low grade on a term paper because she doesn't like the title. When I remind her that it was she who assigned me the title, she slams her books on the table, turns her back.

~ ~ ~

While waiting for Richard to reach the same matrimonial conclusion as mine, I spend the last semester of school in a blur of twenty units of upper division classes in English literature, and psychology.

I am finally eligible to take the one class that completes my reason for my college career, the lab class Intern Teaching.

Dr. Altena, the professor in charge of student teachers, is a recent refugee from Dutch Indonesia. It is she who decides that my internship will be spent teaching American literature to all five classes of juniors at Yankton High School. When I ask to be assigned the seniors who are studying English literature, she brushes my concerns aside. It is unimportant that my major is in English literature. There is no difference between the two subjects, she insists.

Following Dr. Altena's instructions, on the first day of my internship I arrive in the classroom a little before 8:30 a.m. After first period class assembles, my master teacher introduces me and walks briskly from the classroom. I never see her again during my six week tenure as student teacher. I am never shown the teachers lunch room or toilet. Evidently there is no smoking room for staff either. I experience incredible withdrawals from nicotine.

Abandoned, the junior class of Yankton High School and I struggle to survive my six week endurance test-internship.

First period students become alert after the dismissal bell rings.

Second period students have only five minutes in the halls to discover what lesson is being presented for the day. They do not gather enough information to sabotage my lesson plans.

Third period class, ready to undermine the expected lesson, turns surly when I present an entirely different agenda. Lunch hour provides enough time for the entire junior class to compare notes.

Fourth period consists of nineteen juniors who play varsity and junior varsity football and one extremely unhappy girl. Their idea of expressing dissatisfaction with a lesson different from first and third period is to open the windows to a courtyard three stories below, and attempt to throw the chairs down into it.

Commandeering all authority my-five-feet-four-inch-one-hundred-thirty-pound body can muster, I step from behind my desk, grab the closest student, reach up to pick him up by the scruff of his neck, then the seat of his pants, and heave him in the general direction of an undisturbed chair. This course of action effectively halts the advance on the windows. The stories of the effect of adrenalin in a life threatening environment are true.

Fifth period students seem contented to sit calmly for their last class of the day.

During a third period lesson George, a recent transplant from California, surrenders his switchblade after providing me with an unsolicited demonstration on the versatility of his unusual cutlery.

Howard, a fourth period jock, leaps from his chair; writes *fuck this shit* on the blackboard, returns to his seat. I congratulate him on the correct spelling of his message, insist he erase it. At the end of class, his friend takes me aside to ask me please not tell anyone as Howard will just be beaten some more by his father if anyone finds out.

In between skirmishes, the students produce correctly written letters to the Gurney Seed Company ordering the necessary seeds for a spring vegetable garden. The letters pass the scrutiny of the principal. Walt Whitman's poetry, despite his reputation as a sissy, gains respect after the classes read and discuss *The Wound Dresser.*

I use pop quizzes, essay tests, multiple-choice tests as one method of classroom control. The principal interrupts a lesson to tell me I may not give any Fs.

The day before my internship ends, all the students in every class exhibit model behavior. Dr. Altena arrives during fourth period, just in time for a discussion of Walt Whitman's, Bivouac in the Flood. Every hand shoots into the air at every question I ask. Every answer is correctly given. Dr. Altena is as captivated as I am. The bell rings, the doctor leaves, the class lines up, files out the door in unbelievable orderliness. The last student out the door whispers *how'd we do*, grins, continues his sedate exit.

Bedlam reigns in fifth period. *Will you get an A?* one of the students shouts. *We really tried,* another one says.

Their efforts are successful. Dr. Altena rewards me with an A+.

~~~

Somehow, when the semester ends in January, I have completed all the requirements for a Bachelor of Arts degree and a teaching credential.

I pack up my precious books, the rest of my sparse belongings, board the bus for Pierre and the uncharted territory of the newly graduated and unemployed.

I am unable to teach because, one, I cannot face returning to the classroom, no matter which side of the desk I am on and two, I lack the necessary requirement of American citizenship and therefore ineligible for a teaching credential in the state of South Dakota.

~ ~ ~

Edna arranges for me to take a qualifying exam for employment with the Department of Welfare. Although I have no idea what the answers to most of the multiple choice questions are, I somehow am assigned to a position in Watertown. Situated on the shore of Lake Kampeska, Watertown endures cold damp winters, damp hot summers.

~ ~ ~

With my course of study complete, the checks from Dad no longer arrive at the first of every month. Mother and Edna stake me to my new career with a loan of seventy-five dollars.

~ ~ ~

I arrive in Watertown. My supervisor meets me at the bus depot, takes me to the home of a lovely widow where I rent a room for twenty-five dollars a month. The remaining fifty dollars will be used for food and cigarettes and other necessities until my first payday.

~ ~ ~

A small restaurant close to the county courthouse serves three pancakes, butter, syrup, and coffee for twenty-five cents. The first day I patronize the little café, I arouse the owner's mild curiosity by showing up and ordering pancakes for all three meals. After two weeks of faithful appearances, always ordering the same dish, curiosity turns to frank disbelief. After a month of perfect attendance at all three meals, no one will look directly at me as I place my order.

~ ~ ~

While on a field trip to check the water quality of the James River, Richard visits me at the Child Welfare office which is housed in the basement of the county courthouse, next to the county jail. As a gift, he brings me a small carp swimming in the bottom of a mayonnaise jar. He found the fish while checking the purity of the James River. I have no idea where he found the jar. With no place for a wild fish in my life, I flush him down the toilet in hopes he will get back from whence he came.

~ ~ ~

After a few days on the job, I realize that nothing I learned in college has prepared me for the intricacies of welfare work.

~ ~ ~

I take an infant to the pediatrician for a check-up because the foster mother says there is something wrong with him *down there*. The pediatrician glowers at me. *You know perfectly well this baby needs to be circumcised. Don't bring him back into my office until you have the release signed from either his mother or the state.*

The mother will not release her baby to the state for adoption; the state will not approve the cost of the circumcision until the mother releases the baby. Catch 22 exists everywhere.

~ ~ ~

A well-dressed woman hugging a well-dressed baby comes to the office for a social call. The adoption is final, the baby is beautiful, and the entire family is in love with her. The new mother hangs her head in embarrassment. She confesses. She is pregnant. She hopes none of the workers mind. Too elated over the second miracle in her life to care much if they do, she leaves amid a flurry of hugs and kisses.

~ ~ ~

A minister and his wife want desperately to adopt. They have chosen two little Indian girls. The sisters have been made wards of the state after repeated abuse by their alcoholic mother. Policy states that interracial adoptions are too risky for both the parents and the children. The sisters remain in foster care.

~ ~ ~

Richard drives down from Aberdeen to visit during a fierce blizzard even though the sheriff tells me the highways are closed. I am overjoyed with his bravery. He does not ask me to go back to Aberdeen with him.

~ ~ ~

My supervisor sends me out to interview Mr. Fox. The school nurse wants permission to test his children for TB because their mother recently died of the disease. Mr. Fox lives in an unheated one-room shack with his second wife and their assorted children. He stops working on an automobile in his front yard when I arrive. He takes me into his home, which is furnished with one bed. He introduces me to his new wife who speaks no English. After a short conversation in Lakota with his wife, Mr. Fox signs an agreement to allow three of his children to undergo a medical examination. I request that he allow all the children to be tested. Without another word, Mr. Fox lets me know I have pushed his patience to the limit, returns to his interrupted work.

~ ~ ~

Easter Sunday I don my new spring hat to attend services at Trinity Episcopal Church. A fierce snow storms makes me wish I had worn my winter woolen scarf.

~ ~ ~

Sent to Pierre to attend budget hearings at the state legislature, I listen to a state senator who takes the floor to announce that he is not voting for any welfare benefits as there are no needy children in the state of South Dakota.

Back in Watertown, my supervisor assigns me the task of investigating a school nurse's request for free lunch for two of the children attending the elementary school where she provides the only medical attention many of the children receive. A home visit enables me to evaluate the necessity of a government grant for the requested lunches. I knock on the door of a run-down house in a run-down neighborhood. The father answers my knock, warmly welcomes me into the neat, sparsely furnished house. The children, thin and poorly dressed, peer out from behind their thin, poorly dressed mother. The young father explains that he works in construction and jobs are non-existent in the winter. I contact the school nurse to recommend these children receive free lunches.

The next time I see my client, it is a sunny April morning. Under the watchful eye of the sheriff's deputy, he and some of the other county prisoners are weeding the courthouse grounds. *Hi Miss Bruce,* he calls out. I wave back. Dropping by the Sheriff's office, I ask him to explain my client's gardening with the county felons. *He is doing ninety days for selling his landlord's furniture,* is the terse explanation.

~ ~ ~

After I am given my first paycheck, I realize I made more money as a waitress.

~ ~ ~

In contrast to writing term papers, I learn to write a short concise, coherent report of my contacts with clients for the office secretary to type and place in the client's permanent file.

~ ~ ~

I investigate joining the U. S. Navy. I am not eligible. I lack American citizenship.

~ ~ ~

Richard pays his final visit to Watertown in March to tell me good-bye. The Korean Police Action necessitates higher production of the B-36 bomber which has increased the demand for engineers. On his way to Texas to work for Consolidated Vultee Aircraft, Richard stops in Lincoln. Consolidated Vultee Aircraft will also employ Jim as soon as the FBI completes their security check on him. From Lincoln, Richard and Jim follow each other to Fort Worth. Gerry will arrive in Texas with their baby, Todd after decent housing can be found.

To keep myself busy after Richard leaves, I knit him a pair of socks. In his thank you note, he reports that the tops of the socks stop just below his armpits.

I buy a chair seat cover to needlepoint. I don't care that I don't own a chair.

Marion Eskelson

After writing long letters to each other, Richard finally agrees we should marry.

~ ~ ~

I resign my post as probably the worst child welfare worker the state of South Dakota has ever known. Happily, I leave Watertown on Memorial Day. Snow and ice still hug the lakeshore.

Part 5:
Texas: A Tough Trek 1951–1956

June, 1951 I shake the snow from my feet, vow never to return to South Dakota, and board a plane in Sioux Falls heading for Fort Worth, Texas. Arriving at the Amon Carter Airport, I step out of the aircraft and into a wall of heat and the arms of my cool collected fiancé, Richard. From there we drive to my brother's house in Ridgley, a new housing subdivision of Fort Worth close to Consolidated Vultee Aircraft.

Despite a weak economy, Consolidated is hiring engineers to speed the manufacture of the B-36 for the Korean conflict. Jim, waiting for security clearance, works in a local gas station which doesn't need nor appreciate his skills as a mechanical engineer. Richard has already been cleared despite being a civil engineer. He is an American citizen.

With Jim and his degree in mechanical engineering at the gas station and Gerry, his registered-nurse-wife, working for an ob-gyn. I am left to care for their six month old baby. Todd is an unbelievably alert and beautiful baby, blond, and olive skinned, green eyed and, healthy. Starting to eat solids, he prefers fruits to vegetables. But one day after lunch, he has a bad afternoon. I rock and walk, proffer bottles of formula, water, and juice. Nothing works. Gerry arrives home from work. Todd leaps from my arms into hers, puts his head on her shoulder and nods off to sleep. Before I can describe his distress to his mother, he poops. He poops all over her white nurses uniform, all over her legs, her shoes, the kitchen floor, all the while sighing and remaining blissfully asleep on her shoulder. It is from this experience that I learn not ever to give a baby a whole jar of Gerber's prunes for lunch.

Aside from that, I keep the house clean, the laundry up to date, prepare evening meals and send everyone off to work with a lovely brown paper sack filled with nutritious food.

~ ~ ~

During my stint as failed-welfare-worker-turned-manager of a household of refugees from a slow Northern economy, I discover a large bug living in the pots and pans cupboard. I take the strange critter to a neighbor. She identifies it as a cockroach. She also explains the weather. *This is no heat wave, this is summertime in Texas,* she explains.

That night, despite the neighbor's amused advice of live and let live, Gerry and I begin what will be a futile attempt to eradicate this indestructible Texas-sized critter.

~ ~ ~

After the dinner, dishes have been washed and put away, Richard and I have long discussions on the joys and responsibilities of marriage. We set the wedding day for July 14, 1951.

During one serious prenuptial discussion, I solemnly state, *When it comes to that part of the ceremony where I am to say, I promise to love, honor, and obey, I won't mean the "obey". I will say it because it is required. You're the smartest man I have ever met, but you're not smart enough for me to obey.*

Richard seems unruffled by this news.

Emboldened I suggest that we take my maiden name for practical reasons. Bruce, I explain, is much easier to spell than Eskelson. Besides, no one can pronounce Eskelson. Richard remains resolute. Our married name will be Eskelson.

~ ~ ~

Richard takes me shopping at Dillard's, Fort Worth's department store in downtown Fort Worth. The air conditioned store provides an oasis of cool, a rarity in 1951. I suck in the cool dry air. I spy a drinking fountain. *Look*, I exclaim excitedly, *colored water.*

Richard looks at me in disbelief.

Well, look at the sign. It says "colored". I hurry over; press the button to activate the flow of water. Plain water shoots from the faucet. *Aw, it's broken*, I say.

Richard grabs my arm, hisses in my ear, *It's not colored water. It's for colored people.*

I begin to argue with him. After all, it is a fountain and the sign plainly states colored.

He pushes me past a gathering crowd, hustles me out of the store.

Over a beer in a real Texas honky-tonk where a woman makes love to the juke box and over the din of the inmates in the adjacent Tarrant County jail, Richard explains Jim Crow to me.

~~~

Gerry and I go to the Tarrant County courthouse for the wedding certificate. Richard's presence is unnecessary for the purchase, unlike the Wasserman blood test where attendance is mandatory for both parties.

~~~

On a blistering Bastille Day in Fort Worth Texas, Richard and I, along with Jim and Gerry, our witnesses, arrive at the Ridgley Methodist Church. The Protestant Episcopal Church of the United States of America will not marry us as Richard had been briefly married and divorced about six years before we met. The Methodists suffer no such prejudice as to repeat performances of the sacrament of marriage and provide us with another chance at Holy Matrimony. The ceremony lasts long enough for us to take each other for richer and poorer and for me, under duress, to vow obedience. The preacher, in a hurry, looks around like a man who expects to be stiffed until Jim, keeper of the wedding ring, license and accompanying gratuity, asks where he and Gerry sign the wedding certificate. The preacher then explains that no witnesses are needed in Texas. Jim puts the marriage license back in his jacket pocket, hands the preacher the envelope with the obligatory matrimonial fee and we once again return to the outdoors' blinding light and ever present heat.

The preacher scurries off to a revival. We hunt for a restaurant where we can celebrate our nuptials.

~ ~ ~

We honeymoon in Cloudcroft, New Mexico. Driving through western Texas we remark about the constant signs advertising gin mills. Richard doesn't want to stop at some honky-tonk but I insist. I have never been in a gin mill. Night clubs, bars, yes, but never a gin mill. The gin mill turns out to be a place where cotton crops are taken to be rid of their seeds.

I am beginning to feel like I did after being told the correct pronunciation of Pierre when my family moved to South Dakota.

~ ~ ~

We luxuriate in the cool comfort of Cloudcroft, perched in the Sacramento Mountains of New Mexico. The Indians we see dress differently and are much smaller in stature than the Sioux with whom Richard and I went to school. Many have the same dull-eyed defeated look of their northern brothers and sisters.

One morning, I decide to eat a real New Mexican breakfast of *huevos rancheros*. My Anglo body has never known garlic and wishes to experience the novel flavor for as long as possible. As a result, I am encased in an odor that neither toothpaste, perfume, soap nor the ingestion of massive quantities of chlorophyll gum can defeat.

I lock the keys in the car. We only have one set. Richard breaks the little wing window to get in the car.

His patience will be tested by these kinds of experiences until the day he dies.

Both Richard and I decline an invitation to a cock fight. *Lotta fun,* the barkeep assures us.

~ ~ ~

Too soon we leave the coolness of the Sacramento's for the insufferable heat of Forth Worth and our new home. We have rented an apartment from Mrs. Lowe. The economics of widowhood have forced her to enclose her back porch into rentable living space.

Hence our apartment.

This meager space provides a tiny kitchen equipped with a tiny sink, a tiny refrigerator, and a really tiny stove. The leftover space gives way to a Murphy bed. Richard's feet hang over the end of this contraption. A cozy little table with two chairs completes our first home.

We share the bathroom with Mrs. Lowe. Because both Richard and I know dormitory bathroom rules, we experience no conflicts. Mrs. Lowe suffers from some digestive malady that gives new meaning to the term "thunder mug."

~ ~ ~

I file for naturalization papers at the federal courthouse in Fort Worth. The Bureau of Immigration and Naturalization sits tucked away in a recessed corner of the second floor of this august building. For a five dollar fee, I fill out a brief form of intent that demands this basic information; country of origin, date of birth, sex, race, number of years of residence, education, occupation, but most importantly, marital status. While writing a receipt for my filing fee, the clerk asks if I would like to sign up for an education class. I decline, explaining that I have lived in the United States most of my life and received most of my education here. She accepts my refusal with a shrug, hands me my receipt, and says *y'all hurry back.*

~ ~ ~

I find a job in the credit department of Montgomery Ward. I don't speak much Texan and most Texans do not understand my Yankee English.

At lunch, one of the credit department women tells of having to carry her husband to the doctor. She is not a large woman.

My God! I gasp, *what was wrong with him?* It seems he hurt his foot and couldn't drive so she carried him to the doctor.

How far is it from your house to the doctors, I ask, incredulity falling from every syllable.

Oh, she says crushing her corn bread into her glass of buttermilk. *I carried him in the car.*

You're teasing me, I say. *How could you carry him in the car?*

She becomes agitated. *How do you carry anyone in a car? I drove and he sat in the back seat with his foot propped up.* She eyes me with suspicion.

Thus begins my learning Texan as a second language.

An elderly Negro approaches my window. Truly incapable of understanding him I say, *Sir I don't seem able to help you. If you will just step over to the desk next to mine, the clerk there will help you.*

The clerk sitting next to me says, *Don't call him "sir"!*

But I don't know his name, I tell her.

Call him "boy", she snaps.

I am flabbergasted. *Why would I call him "boy"? He's an old man,* I protest.

No one sits with me during lunch break.

~ ~ ~

After constant but unsuccessful attempts, I finally become pregnant. I happily quit my job in the Montgomery Ward' credit office to the relief of almost everyone there.

~ ~ ~

In the fullness of time, a letter from the Bureau of Immigration and Naturalization summons me to an interview with a naturalization officer. I will need two witnesses to swear that I will be a loyal American citizen. I enlist Mrs. Lowe and Ginny Graham. Ginny qualifies as a witness because her husband went to the South Dakota State School of Mines and Technology at the same time Richard did. Mrs. Lowe qualifies because my husband pays her the rent promptly.

On the day of my appointment I don my best maternity skirt and smock, and Ginny picks up Mrs. Lowe and me. Together we drive downtown to the court house. Upon arrival on the second floor, my witnesses are detained on a bench in the hall. I am ushered into the small office of the officer in charge of naturalization.

The naturalization officer stands and opens a thick folder on his desk. I swear under oath that everything I say will be true. He then motions me to sit in a chair opposite his desk.

My interrogation begins.

State your full name, please.

Mrs. Richard J. Eskelson

Your name is Richard? he sneers.

I listen as he explains the differences between social and legal names

We then enter into a lively discussion as to my citizenship. I insist that I am a Canadian citizen to no avail. After checking my dossier he announces that I am a citizen of Great Britain.

The hour and a half interview continues pretty much along these lines. He tells me I have a poor understanding of American history and civics. I remind him that I was educated in the United States.

I manage to convince him that neither Job's Daughters nor Senior Girl Scouts is a Communist organization.

He threatens to deport me because I can't find my green cards. After Mother's death, we will find them tucked away among her treasured mementos.

I explain how I will be able to vote in the upcoming election with or without his permission. I show him my recently purchased poll tax. He stands up, leaves the room briefly. When he returns he tells me that my witnesses do not qualify and I will need eight people to write a recommendation for my admittance to full citizenry of the United States of America. He leaves the room.

I have been dismissed.

I comply with his unrealistic demand that I have eight witnesses agree I am a safe person to become a voting citizen of the United States. I send letters to many college professors and high school teachers. Evidently a sufficient number of professors and teachers honor my request but I won't know that until I am notified to appear at the swearing in ceremony.

~~~

Mrs. Lowe turns out to be a wonderful landlady. She had only heard about damnyankees before she rented her porch-cum-apartment to us. She decided to take a chance after she met Richard. *He is so sweet and nice looking*, she tells me.

One brisk fall day she asks me whether I like chrystillanthiums. *I certainly do*, I say.

I'm especially fond of the big ones they wear to the football games, aren't you? is her next question.

I agree with her again.

Richard comes home from work and she knocks on our door. *My radio doesn't work very well. I think it needs a transfusion, and I wonder if you would look at it*, she asks Richard. He examines her small and really old portable radio and disappoints her when he tells her he doesn't think a new anything will help.

When Richard gets the flu she inquires as to his health every day, bringing him black eyed peas and hush puppies. She wonders if he has gone to the doctor for some wonder drugs. *That penericillium and sulfer work miracles, I understand,* she says.

She tells me of her nephew, who was accepted at the University of Chicago, and when he went to class a nigger came in and sat right next to him and he just got up and left and went to Texas Christian instead. I agree it was probably the best thing for everyone, including the universities.

On a bright, warm December day, she inquires as to my obvious sadness. *Well, I tell her, it is so hot and it just doesn't seem like Christmas.* She smiles. *Honey,* she says, *what makes you think Jesus was born in a snow storm?*

When Mrs. Lowe realizes that Richard's feet hang over the Murphy bed, she provides us with a longer version of a Murphy.

~ ~ ~

She offers us her home so that we can invite people over for our first Thanksgiving dinner. She will be spending the day with her daughter's family. We accept her invitation.

I have never cooked a turkey before.

Don't worry, Jim's wife tells me, *there's nothing to it. I'll be over to help you.*

Richard and I are up early to begin this most important of meals. Eight guests have been invited.

I struggle with stuffing the turkey after Richard has struggled to clean it. By some miracle the bird fits in the oven.

Richard helps peel the potatoes. We use frozen peas as they are not only a delicacy, they are also a novelty.

We chose two o'clock for dinner time. We set the table using Mrs. Lowe's flatware, dishes and tablecloth. About noon Richard begins to wonder aloud if the turkey will be done by two. By one o'clock, we decide it will not be done if we keep opening the oven door to see how well it is cooking.

Jim, Gerry, and Todd arrive about 1:55 with the sweet potatoes. We sit down to dinner with the rest of the guests about 2:25. Everyone proclaims it a most excellent meal.

~ ~ ~

Richard and Jim are working on a patent that will revolutionize medicine; something about the way IVs are administered.

One morning before leaving for work Richard hands me the car keys with written instructions as how to get to an industrial part of Fort Worth. There, I will be able to purchase the paraphernalia needed to build a model of their machine.

Once the model is designed, patented, and in production, we will be rich, rich, rich.

~ ~ ~

I have never driven a car in my life. The Studebaker has an automatic transmission. There will be no problems, Richard assures me. He leaves for work in his car pool.

I proceed with my wifely duties and set out to find and bring home industrial strength, clear, plastic tubing.

The streets in old Fort Worth, twisted and narrow, follow trails the cowboys used when they drove their herds to the railhead.

Richard's directions do not explain why people honk angrily at me on some of the streets even though I get as close to the curb as I can. Too many cars sit parked on just one side of these narrow passageways for safe driving, anyway.

As hard as I try to follow Richard's well intentioned directions, I realize that somehow I have gotten lost. I find myself driving on a really large road with many lanes, as the city of Dallas looms closer and closer. At least the sign says the upcoming city is Dallas.

A large grassy median separates eastbound traffic from westbound. I know if I get into Dallas I will never find my way back to Fort Worth. I make a U turn across all the lanes on the road, bump over the grassy median and end up on the roadway that leads west, and back to Fort Worth.

I petition the Almighty: *Get me back home and I will never drive this way again.* My plea is granted. I keep my promise.

I successfully complete my first driving lesson.

~ ~ ~

A few days later Jim calls. He has succumbed to the heat. Full of newly born confidence, I pick him up and we begin the ride back home. Once again I run across an irritated driver who rudely honks his horn. Jim sits up, observes the situation and roars, *For Christ's sake, are you trying to kill us?*

When we safely arrive home, he explains the meaning of the arrow on a *One Way* sign.

I successfully complete my second driving lesson.

~ ~ ~

March, 1952, Barbara calls me from her home in Rapid City. Grandfather has been in a terrible car accident. He ran into a bridge abutment on his way from Pierre to Rapid City to visit her and his great-grandchildren. He was found by a highway patrolman who took him to the four bed hospital in Quinn where the doctor treated his wounds. He has lost his left eye, torn several ribs from his sternum, bitten through his upper lip and although his great long legs are not broken, they are badly abraded.

Come home as soon as you can Barbara says. *Grandfather has developed pneumonia. No one expects him to survive this latest car wreck.*

Despite being three months pregnant, I board the Greyhound bus. After two days of wandering through the grasslands of America, I arrive in Pierre, South Dakota. Because no public transportation is available,

Mother's friend drives me the final 112 miles to Quinn. I hurry in to Grandfather's hospital room. He looks terrible. His breathing is labored. In spite of the morphine, he is in pain. I take his bony, old hand and kiss him on his forehead ,the only place that is not black and blue. *I'm here, Grandfather*, I tell him. *I love you.*

He opens his eyes. They flood with tears. He grasps my hand tightly and coughs through the agony of his torn chest. By some miracle, his cough is productive. He eases himself back onto his pillow. *My girl,* he whispers through his pain, I *have to tell you something.* He pulls me close.

Grandfather, I reassure him, *everything is fine. I'm here to stay with you; the doctor is doing a good job.* My knees feel weak. I do not want to hear his deathbed confession.

I'm worried, he gasps. *I'm afraid that I will never drive a car again.*

Ten days after the accident Grandfather walks out of the hospital climbs into Barbara's car and we drive the sixty miles from Quinn to Rapid City. We deposit him in Saint John's hospital. After two days of x-rays and more examinations, we take him to the airport where he boards a plane for Pierre. He is eighty three years old.

Clara, a friend of the family, makes the observation that the Good Lord called J. B. but J. B. wasn't ready to go.

~ ~ ~

Richard calls Barbara's house with news. *Come home* he says. *We're moving to Austin. I have a job with a construction company.*

Barbara and I look up Austin in her atlas. It is farther south than Fort Worth. *Maybe its cooler there,* Barbara says.

~ ~ ~

We move to Austin. We have no difficulty packing all our belongings in our spiffy Studebaker with its automatic transmission.

Because Richard works as an apprentice for a registered engineer, he earns apprentice wages. We have enough money to pay rent for an apartment above a garage on a tree lined Austin street with enough left over to buy food, cigarettes, and make the car payment.

Mrs. Lindamood is our new landlady. May is lovely in Austin. I take a blanket and lie out in the sun. After a few minutes, Mrs. Lindamood approaches. She has been watching me from her kitchen window.

Honey, she says, standing so as to block the sun from my body. *You don't want to be out here, really.*

I tell her I enjoy the sun and her lovely backyard.

Well honey, she says softly, *I think you better go in now. You don't want your baby to be born dark.*

Her stern request finds me retreating back into the safety of my shaded apartment.

~ ~ ~

A mom and pop grocery sits across the street from the apartment. I can buy a watermelon for fifteen cents. I hurry to make my purchase early in the morning. By afternoon I eat chilled watermelon to ease myself through the 115 degree afternoon heat.

~ ~ ~

The United States Government invites me to appear at a swearing in ceremony for newly accepted petitioners for full United States citizenship. Friday, June 13, 1952 arrives hotter than hot. Richard takes the day off and we leave Austin early in order to arrive at the Fort Worth federal courthouse by 10:00a.m. Richard is not allowed in the courtroom as he is not dressed properly in jacket and tie. A retired judge from Maryland sings a quavery rendition of "Oh Maryland, My Maryland", says the U. S. allows for religious differences and swears all candidates for citizenship to forsake all former fealties to king and/or country and promise to defend the Constitution of the United States against all enemies, foreign and domestic. I do eagerly so swear.

My naturalization papers state I was a citizen of Great Britain.

~ ~ ~

On the other hand, the process by which Barbara achieved full citizenship lacked any formality. The naturalization officer in Rapid City shook her hand, said he was glad to see her, gave her an American flag, said she would be notified about the swearing in ceremony, and congratulated her on her decision. Jim's admission to full citizenship was equally as casual. Both he and Barbara's papers state that they were citizens of Canada.`

~ ~ ~

One insufferable, hot, humid August evening I am brushing my teeth when out of the bathroom sink crawls a toothpaste and spit encrusted creature. I watch in horror as it climbs out of the drain, up the side of the sink, over the edge, splats onto the floor and continues its journey across the bathroom tiles unmindful of my screams. Retching, I rush to where the broom is kept and vainly attempt to kill this large slow moving bug recently housed in the Austin sewer. My hitting it repeatedly with the broom does not deter its progress. Richard watches the battle until it ceases to amuse him. He finds the dustpan, takes the broom from my tiring arms, sweeps up the bug, throws it out the front door, and replaces the broom and dust pan to their assigned places in the kitchen. Then he tries to quiet my incessant demands that he get me the hell out of here.

On August 31, Mother and Auntie Edna call ostensibly to wish Richard a happy birthday.

When it is my turn to talk, Mother asks me if I have had the baby. I burst into tears. *I'm going to be pregnant the rest of my life,* I wail. *I'm going to apply for permanent disability. I'm too huge to move and it is too hot to breathe.* I sob loudly.

Richard gently removes the phone from my hand, reassures both Mother and Edna that I am fine, just tired of being pregnant in August in Texas.

Six days later, in the midst of the first rainstorm in months, I am delivered of a seven pound, eight ounce boy. The delivery was uneventful although throughout the entire labor, I kept telling Richard that I had changed my mind and he should take me home. The demurral probably had something to do with my irrelevant demands.

James David is a perfectly lovely baby. He has a full head of dark brown hair, all the necessary fingers and toes and startling blue eyes.

All babies have blue eyes, the nurse says.

Nice job, Richard says.

We receive a congratulatory telegram from Richard's parents. Jamie is the first male Eskelson grandchild and the proud grandparents are really pleased with me.

Much to the disapproval of the doctor and the hospital staff, I insist on nursing this most wonderful of babies.

Damnyankees seem ignorant of the fact that nice white ladies don't nurse their babies; they hire black women to wet nurse.

When we leave the hospital everyone says, *y'all hurry back.*

Mrs. Lindamood announces that she doesn't allow children in her apartment.

We begin a search for some place where all three of us can be comfortably housed. I am glad to say good-bye to the long climb up the stairs, to the enormous water bugs that crawl up through the bathroom sink, to the man next door who, in the early morning hours, shoots at the birds in his tree whose branches shade our bedroom window.

We find a rental in one of the new subdivisions in Austin, a one bath, two bedroom house on a cul-de-sac created to give the newness of the development an elegant touch. The cul-de-sac is as sun baked and barren as our backyard. We move in, only to discover some startling differences between the standard housing of South Dakota and Texas. No insulation is to be found anywhere in this new house, not even in the attic. Central heating consists of a natural gas nozzle in each room. A natural gas burning portable heater comes equipped with a rubber hose that connects to the various nozzles.

Both Richard and I worry about the safety of this unusual heating arrangement especially after Jamie learns to crawl, discovers this fascinating appliance, pulls the hose from the nozzle, and turns the gas on and off, just for fun.

Texans describe a "Blue Norther" as a winter wind that blows down from the North Pole with nothing between it and Texas but a barbed wire fence. When a Blue Norther hits, I put extra clothes on Jamie and myself, stay in the kitchen where the stove keeps the room warm, pile every blanket we own on the bed at night, and watch condensing moisture drip down the walls. Some of the red dirt escapes the accompanying sleet. Suddenly, everything enjoys a rosy coating of sand. I cough. Jamie develops pneumonia. The doctor prescribes asthma medicine, and antibiotics for him.

After I become acquainted with one of the neighbors, I ask why none of the houses are insulated. Mary looks at me with renewed interest. *Honey,* she says, *you don't want to keep all the summer heat in do you?*

Get me the hell out of here! I plead with Richard.

～～～

Mary, proud owner of a large, flourishing garden, grows a variety of vegetables. Spinach, green beans, pinto beans, tomatoes and okra flourish under her care. She grows no corn because corn takes up too much space, she explains. We both agree that nothing tastes better than vegetables picked fresh and cooked for the evening meal. She picks spinach early in the morning before the sun can burn it, washes it thoroughly, puts it in a large pot full of water, simmers it until time for six o'clock dinner. Okra, green beans, pinto beans, no matter what the vegetable, all are cooked in the same time honored method.

When she bakes a turkey she first scrubs the bird inside and out, puts it in a large pot, covers it with water, simmers it for a couple of hours, takes it out of the water, lets it cool, stuffs it with corn bread, puts it in a roaster pan, adds the water in which it has been simmered, and puts the roaster in the oven. When the water is mostly evaporated, she removes the roasting pan from the oven and makes gravy with the drippings.

When frying bacon she first dredges the slices in flour, fries them slowly in a large skillet, and makes gravy with the drippings. *Otherwise, you'd loose the fat,* she explains to me.

~~~

Mary graciously invites me to lunch with several other ladies. She serves us a lovely meal which includes canned green peas. After the meal we are invited into the front room for coffee. The woman who was seated to my left at the table excuses herself, goes to the kitchen, and returns with one of the empty cans that had held the green peas. She seats herself next to me on the sofa.

I would like to invite you to my church on Sunday, she says.

How kind of you, I say. *But I have a spiritual home.*

What might that be? She seems confused by my answer.

I go to the little Episcopal mission just a few blocks from here. Saint George's. Perhaps you know where it is, I tell her.

She draws herself up, and leaning into my face, hisses through her teeth, *Whiskeypalian! Whiskeypalian are you? If it weren't for you damned Whiskeypalians, Texas would be a dry state.* She spits a stream of tobacco juice into the once empty green pea can.

When Richard comes home from work that evening, I meet him at the door. *Get me the hell out of here,* I demand through clenched teeth.

~~~

It is in this little spot of southwestern America where I will learn just how uninformed I am of cultural differences between North and South.

Ham is always boiled to remove the excess salt.

No one puts either butter or margarine on their bread.

No one eats Boston baked beans.

Everyone eats pinto beans boiled with salt pork.

For good luck, on New Year's Day, everyone eats black eyed peas accompanied by deep fried hush puppies.

The banks are closed on Jefferson Davis's birthday, open on Lincoln's. *But Jefferson Davis was a traitor*, I gasp.

Damnyankee is an epithet not kindly meant. On a bad day I once more am called a damnyankee. My manners disintegrate in the Texas heat. *You know*, I tell the snarling Texan, *my great-granddaddy fought the damnyankees too only his side won and he was given a silver medal by Queen Victoria.* The taunts cease, at least in that neighborhood.

~ ~ ~

Across the road lives the Negro community. Denied ownership of property, they keep their rented yards tidy and massed with blooms, drive large cars. If I want help I just cross the road and knock any door. If no one at that house needs a job, I return home. Soon a woman arrives at my door ready to perform whatever household task I ask of her for fifty cents per hour.

You watch those folk, I am told. *They tote, especially food.*

I never have anything stolen.

I begin to develop friendships with my neighbors across the road.

~ ~ ~

Richard has a poor concept of matrimonial finance. I am not to ask for money. If he thinks I need money he will give me some.

We discuss the distribution of money between married people.

Do you remember I was working and going to school when you met me?

Yes.

Do you remember my telling you I went to school and worked when I was in high school?

Yes.

Richard, I've been handling my own money since I was thirteen years old.

What does that have to do with it? You don't need any money now that we're married. If you need something, I will see you get it.

Are you crazy?

That is how my mother and dad did it. If she needed groceries, she had a charge at the grocery store and she couldn't go over the limit. If my mother needed a dress, my dad gave her the money and she bought herself a dress.

I remind him of previous discussions about his mother, her coffee making in particular. *I asked you if I looked like your mother and you said no and I said well, I don't make coffee like she does either. You knew I could read and write before we were married. Jesus did not ask me to leave my brains on the altar of matrimony. And before you leave for work, take a good look at the color of my skin. I don't look like your nigger either.*

I sing *Got along without ya before I met ya, gonna get along without ya now.*

Richard pours himself another cup of coffee, lights a cigarette and gives the morning paper a more careful reading.

My temper tantrum does nothing to change his opinion that a married woman is incapable of handling money.

~~~

In Texas, a woman cannot spend over fifty dollars without her husband's written consent.

Across the road sits a small grocery store. I take the check book and Jamie with me to go shopping. I make sure I purchase nothing over three dollars, sign the check Mrs. Richard J. Eskelson, the owner extends the courtesy of honoring the check. I do this repeatedly.

Payday, and Richard goes to the bank to deposit his paycheck. The teller hands him a signature card and tells him to please have me sign it as they need a copy of my signature at the bank, just to make things legal.

~ ~ ~

I am pregnant again. The doctor is not pleased.

Well, a train goes by every night about 2:30 a.m. and it wakes us, I explain.

The doctor rolls his eyes.

~ ~ ~

Dad writes. Never having been in Texas, he will be visiting us early in November. We haven't corresponded regularly since he stopped sending me college money. Actually, I haven't heard from him since he called me from Calgary urging me not to marry a divorced man, his only contribution to my nuptials.

Upon his arrival, he and Jamie form a mutual adoration society.

Mary, my mentor and advisor for the strange culture in which I find myself, finds Dad to be a fascinating novelty. He is not a damnedyankee but a bona fide war hero who tells fascinating stories. Mary takes Dad on a tour of the Gulf of Mexico where he eats more shrimp than he thought humanly possible and for less money than he thought humanly possible.

We take Dad to El Matamoras, the best Mexican restaurant in Texas. He eats far more tortillas and drinks far more beer than would be good for a man twice his size.

I go into labor. Dick takes me to the hospital. Dad takes care of Jamie and the house until I come back home. Upon my return, Dad leaves for South Dakota and Barbara's house and a less harried environment.

~ ~ ~

This delivery is complicated. I have a postpartum hemorrhage. I have a bicornuate uterus. The baby is on one side, the placenta on the other. I cannot deliver the placenta. Another doctor is called in.

The blood transfusions he orders make me unbelievably ill. Since I am too weak to nurse the baby, my breasts engorge. Richard goes to the drugstore to get ice packs. He returns with one ice pack. *Have you ever noticed I have two of those things on my chest* I ask? We both decide to laugh.

Jamie is fifteen months old.

Richard takes his vacation time to be with us.

I cry when he goes back to work at the end of two weeks.

Don't do this again!, the doctor states emphatically.

~ ~ ~

Carla is a most beautiful baby. She arrives wreathed in blonde curls, with blue eyes and a perfect little body. We name her after her grandfather Eskelson. We do not receive a congratulatory telegram this time.

~ ~ ~

Shortly after Carla's birth the landlord announces he is selling the house. The house next door is conveniently for rent. We move in easily except for a couple of problems. We have no furniture but for the baby crib and bassinet. We don't have much money either. Directed to a reputable second hand store, we buy a gas stove that boasts three out of four functioning burners. The oven heats the kitchen but lacks an accurate thermostat. The refrigerator keeps the milk cool. We buy a secondhand mattress. The bedstead will have to wait. The secondhand man throws in a chest of drawers for free. For less than one hundred dollars, we have become a bona fide household.

~ ~ ~

The colors of the rooms in our new home present a challenge. The front room shouts in bright chartreuse, the kitchen resembles a cave done in deep plum, the bathroom boasts a forest green, and the children's bedroom prevents sleep with its fire engine red decor. Our bedroom, a pale baby blue, somehow fell from the color wagon. We take up residence in our bedroom after the owner indignantly dismisses our offer to paint the walls.

~ ~ ~

In due time, Richard brings home a large sheet of plywood and two pipes. He turns them into a table. He rounds off the sharp edges of the plywood sheet so as not to injure the children and adds a coat of sturdy varnish. He bends the pipes to curve at the correct length, using the plumbing to produce the correct curvature in the pipe. With some hardware magic he fastens the pipes to the bottom of the table's top. Voila! A table.

We make a return trip to the secondhand store and come home with a bedstead and four chairs.

Richard continues to work for apprentice wages.

I develop a reputation as an amazing cook.

~ ~ ~

I don't feel well. I throw up every afternoon. My weight drops to 114 pounds. The heat is unending. We have a swamp cooler but it only works when the humidity is low. Any housework to be done is done before 11:00 a.m. or after 5:00 p.m.

But Richard comes home from work every day, changes his clothes, and takes the children so that I can fix dinner, I tell the doctor. *Then after dinner he either bathes the kids or puts them to bed or he does the dishes or sometimes both.*

It doesn't matter. No more window washing, no more floor scrubbing until your two babies are in school, the doctor admonishes. He writes me a prescription for the latest mother's-little-helper.

With chemical help I stop throwing up, am able to eat and sleep in spite of the heat and humidity.

~ ~ ~

A neighbor stops by for coffee. *What in the world are your children doing?* she asks.

Making cookies for Santa Claus, I explain. *They take turns using my rolling pin to turn graham crackers into crumbs on the kitchen floor. Cookies for Santa!*

But this is July, is her puzzled observation.

She drinks her coffee quickly and leaves.

~ ~ ~

I learn to pray for hurricanes. I don't care if the entire Gulf coast is washed out to sea. Because of those hurricanes, the weather in Austin cools to comfortable.

~ ~ ~

Richard gets a raise after I repeatedly suggest that we move to Kansas where I understand they pay wages in United States currency instead of Texas peanuts.

~ ~ ~

We buy a new stove. The oven door has a see-through window.

Thanksgiving Day Jamie sits in front of the stove all day watching the turkey turn from dead white to tantalizing brown. When it is time for dinner the turkey, placed on a platter, is carried to the homemade table with great fanfare. Richard picks up the knife and begins to carve our festive fowl.

Don't, screams Jamie. *Don't kill the bird, Daddy.*

~ ~ ~

We celebrate Christmas of 1954 with the purchase of a television. The portable set boasts a 12 inch screen encased in black and white composition particle board. We splurge and buy the wrought iron stand. We enjoy the one channel available for viewing in Austin.

~ ~ ~

Richard goes to Houston for a bid opening. He and some other engineers drive from Austin to Houston in a company car. He leaves early in the morning. When he isn't home by 8:00 pm, I begin to get nervous. Houston is the murder capitol of the world and has the highest number of auto related deaths in the United States. By 10:00

p.m. I am convinced I have become a destitute widow with two small children to raise. I lock all the doors and quietly cry myself to sleep.

About midnight I waken when our car pulls into the driveway. Because no one ever locks their doors, Richard has no need to carry a key. He quietly knocks on the front door, rattles the doorknob, knocks on the back door, rattles that doorknob and shortly thereafter, the window in our bedroom is pushed up. Richard, preceded by his great long legs, crawls in through the window and whispers, *Yoo hoo, Mary, I'm a burglar.*

After he leaves the bedroom, I leap from bed, shove the bed against the door, knock the damned gas jet open in the process, slam the window shut, search in the dark for the handle to turn off the hissing gas jet, fall into bed sobbing wildly.

The next evening at dinner I suggest to Richard that if he is ever gone away to Houston or any other place for that matter he should take a couple of minutes to call me just to let me know where he is.

No one else called his wife, he explains.

You aren't married to one of the other wives, I remind him.

~ ~ ~

Ted and Anne, a young couple with a lovely boxer dog moves in next door. We soon become acquainted with them because early one morning, Carla crawls out of her bed, toddles next door and crawls into their bed. Jamie coaxes their dog Max, to play in our back yard while they work selling real estate. One day they come to us with a deal we can't refuse. They have found a lovely house in an older subdivision that they will sell to us at a good price and we can keep the dog when we move.

We move to Palo Duro Drive. The house is perfect except that it isn't insulated either. A large screened back porch, a small fenced back yard, a side yard with a clothes line, a tiny kitchen, two bedrooms, a den and a front room-dining room complete the house. The bathrooms are confusing. The house enjoys the usual bathroom, but a toilet housed in an unlit, windowless room abuts the carport. Although the toilet enjoys proper plumbing, it shows no recent sign of use. Perhaps it is for children when they are outside and in a hurry and don't have time to come inside the house, we reason.

~ ~ ~

Now that we are housed in a middle class house with appropriately painted walls, Richard suggests we invite one of the men he works with and his wife to dinner. We make all the necessary arrangements. We agree that dinner should begin at 6:30 p.m. We have learned never to ask anyone over to the house in the evening because evening means anytime after noon.

Our guests arrive at 10:30p.m. to a ruined dinner.

Richard suggests we invite a different co-worker and his wife. Turkey is cheap. I fix a roast turkey dinner with all the appropriate side dishes. Don raves about the turkey, the dressing, the mashed potatoes, the sweet potatoes, the gravy, and the coffee. He has two pieces of pie. During dinner, Juanita eats less and less until dessert time rolls around. She refuses both pie and coffee. Mute toward the end of the meal, she refuses to answer even a direct question. Our hospitality is never reciprocated.

Had Dante ever visited Texas, there would be eight levels of Hell, I inform Richard.

~ ~ ~

The company appoints Richard as engineer for the construction of the new high school. This contract is a prestigious one. Usually either an engineer or a superintendent manages a job. Being asked to work with an experienced superintendent requires that Richard possess considerable diplomatic skill. Before long a consultation about problems with the concrete pours becomes necessary.

We're being short weighed, Richard insists. The superintendent becomes edgy. To accuse the concrete company of cheating is a serious charge. Much discussion ensues. The problem ends up in the office where Mr.

Morton, chief engineer, and Jamie Odom, the owner, make a decision to gamble on Richard's data. An independent weigh substantiates the accuracy of his figures.

Richard becomes the company hero. Austin is a small town and word travels fast that the young damnyankee engineer knows what he is doing.

The company rewards Richard with a raise. I become pregnant again.

~ ~ ~

The Texas social ladder has many steps. The white, born again, wealthy, professional male occupies the top step. Next on the ladder of acceptance stands his white wife who bears him sons. The third step supports the white wife who has either daughters or no children. Most folk just work, take care of their children, and swear by Billy Graham. This main group fills the middle rung. White trash finds themselves on the next to last step. After that, colored people and Mexicans vie for the bottom step.

~ ~ ~

Janet, a neighbor whom I have never met, rings my doorbell one morning. She wants to borrow a can of tuna. I invite her in and give her the can of tuna. Next, she requests a loaf of bread. I share my loaf of bread with her. She seems encouraged with my generosity. *I need just a little mayonnaise,* she says. She just happens to have a small jar with her. I fill it with mayonnaise. She thanks me profusely. I see her go next door where she collects some lettuce and pickles. She then returns home.

I ask Mary about the strange behavior.

Don't you give her anything next time she comes around begging. That family is nothing but white trash. Her husband works and he never gives her any money for anything. She's invited her mother over for lunch today, that's why she needs the tuna and stuff.

~ ~ ~

President Eisenhower has taken Senator McCarthy aside and stifled the hunt to rid the United States of Communists.

~ ~ ~

Bascom Giles, state treasurer, on trial for embezzlement, is found guilty by a jury of his peers. Sent to Huntsville, he becomes comptroller of the prison after a short stay.

~ ~ ~

Murder seems to be legal in Texas. In the early morning hours, a man in one of the older sections of Austin shoots the paper boy to death. I am horrified. *How could he do that?* I ask Martha, a neighbor.

The boy was trespassing, she explains. *No one can walk on your property without your permission.*

But it was six in the morning and the boy was trying to get the paper on the steps. I quote from the morning edition reporting of the incident.

He should have asked permission from the owner of the house first. Period. End of sentence. She turns and leaves.

A young soldier from Travis Air Base goes out on a date and becomes lost. He pulls into a driveway to ask directions. The owner of the property comes out with a shotgun and blows the young colored man's head off, then steps back in his house and calls the police. No charges are pressed as the young man had not asked permission to be on the owner's property.

A young man breaks into a motel, shoots to death his mother's paramour, and then calmly calls the police. In Texas it is legal to kill the lover but not the wife. The young man had acted on behalf of his father.

Do you know that General Sherman said if he owned Texas and Hell, he would rent Texas and live in Hell? Get me out of here, I scream at Richard when he comes home that evening.

I'm trying to, he replies.

~ ~ ~

185

The Supreme Court rules that segregated education is just separate, not equal. Texans don't have a lot of trouble with that decision. Some grumble but the University of Texas has admitted Negroes in the past. The concern most commonly expressed is that high school children are being thrown in together.

Willie Reen, the young Negro girl who works for me once a week, has been chosen to attend Steven F. Austin High School. No ugly incidents happen when she arrives on campus. She wonders how to overcome the two year lag in her studies. She just knows she cannot fail her family, her church, her community.

Her increased studies leave her no time to work for me. She sends her cousin as a replacement.

~ ~ ~

Time to get your driver's license, Richard announces on my twenty-fifth birthday.

You mean I need a driver's license to drive? I ask. In South Dakota all one needs to drive is a car.

Insurance rates drop in Texas when one reaches twenty-five years of age.

Richard gives me a Texas Division of Motor Vehicles guide to passing the driving exam. I study the rules of the road arduously.

One intensely hot October morning I drive the car to the Department of Motor Vehicles. Once inside, I give the receptionist three dollars and she gives me a pencil and a very large exam book. It takes me over an hour to answer all the questions. When I hand the book back to the receptionist, she asks me to be seated.

After a short wait, an examiner calls my name and we walk to my car. I get in on the driver's side.

He struggles to squeeze in on the passenger's side.

Start the car, please, he says.

Drive to the end of the block, please.

Turn right, please.

Turn right at the end of the block, please.

Turn right at the end of the block, please.

One more right turn, please.

Stop the car, please.

Congratulations, ma'am, your license will be sent to you in the mail.

He exits the passenger side after much pushing, sighing and pushing. He closes the door, walks back to the DMV office. Having completed my formal driver's education, I start the car and drive home legally.

~ ~ ~

Max, our purloined boxer, turns into my best friend. He sleeps in the doorway to my bedroom when Richard is out of town, guards the trash so well that we have to secure him in the bathroom on trash day. He will not allow Carla or Jamie to go out the front door. In his role as lap dog and with each passing month of my pregnancy, he finds it harder and harder to find any room on my lap to cuddle.

~ ~ ~

Stung by a scorpion that was hiding in the couch on the back porch, I inform Richard that I am not going to be his wife anymore, not until he gets me out of this subdivision of Hell. I remove my wedding ring and throw it as far as I can into the hot sticky Texas night. Two days later the next door neighbor knocks on my door, hands me my ring and says that one of her children found it in their backyard. I thank her and wonder aloud how it ever managed to get there.

~ ~ ~

Summer, 1954 and polio continues to devastate its victims. No one uses the public pools, goes to movies, nor shops for anything but essentials. It is during this outbreak that Jim, now living in Dallas, develops a mild case of polio. He and Gerry and Todd moved to Dallas shortly after we moved to Austin. Jim has a job with Ingersol-Rand, Jerry a job with a heart specialist. We will visit back and forth until Ingersol-Rand moves him to North Dakota.

~ ~ ~

When the company puts a bid together, the engineers stay in the office until 11:00 or 12:00 at night. Richard comes home tired and hungry. After several ruined meals, I announce from now on the kitchen is closed at 7:00 p.m. *If that place where you work is so inefficient that it needs you there all those extra hours then they can damned well go buy you a sandwich for supper.* Richard reluctantly agrees after explaining that no company wife has ever refused to fix supper before.

~ ~ ~

A new subdivision of all electrical homes is being offered for sale to the public by Westinghouse. Ronald Reagan serves as spokesman for this most up-to-date housing.

Richard, invited to the opening of the model home, asks me to accompany him on a tour of this advancement in living. Among other technological advancements, every room enjoys air conditioning except for the relatively small kitchen.

Who designed this house anyway? I ask Richard. *If any room ever needed cooling off it's the kitchen.*

If you live in this house you will have not only a maid but also a cook, he whispers.

After Milton spent a month in Texas, he went back home and wrote Paradise Lost, I whisper back.

~ ~ ~

Sometimes when a Blue Norther hits, I go outside barefooted and wearing shorts to tromp through the layer of red ice covering the grass in the front lawn. I experience feeling cold for the first time in weeks. Neighbors no longer wonder about the sanity of damnyankees.

~ ~ ~

The doctor is not pleased with my third pregnancy in less than three years. *You have a choice* he tells me. *Either get some help full time or stay in the hospital for a month after the baby is born.* I give Richard the news. He gets a second job at night, puts the money into a special account; I begin to look for reliable help.

~ ~ ~

Salk's newly developed polio vaccine becomes available in Austin in the latter months of 1955. Because of Jim's experience, the doctor reluctantly agrees to inoculate my pregnant self as well as Jamie and Carla with the rare vaccine.

~ ~ ~

Mother seems disgusted with the news that another grandchild is on the way. *Can't you and Richard think of something else to do?* she tersely comments.

~ ~ ~

Easter Sunday and April Fool's day fall on the same day in 1956. Jamie and Carla complete their Easter egg hunt. Jamie runs to the front door, opens it wide and yells, *Hey Easter Bunny, you forgot the baby.*

~ ~ ~

On April 2, Eula arrives to work for us. The children are happy to have her in their lives. She sings to them, reads them books at nap time and makes sure the ice cream man stops so that they can get a Popsicle. She washes, irons and keeps the house spick-and-span. All I have to do is deliver the baby.

Every morning when she arrives she greets me with, *Miss Mary Anne, you still here?* We strike a bargain. She will teach me how to fry chicken if I will teach her how to make a pie. I learn the secrets of fried chicken. She never does get the hang of a pie crust.

At lunch one day, seated between the two children she says, *Miss Mary Anne, how old is dat little child?* She points to Jamie.

He's three and a half, Eula.

Um hum, Eula says *And how old is dis little child?* She points to Carla.

She's just a little over two, Eula.

Eula shakes her head slowly, puts down her fork, eyes my ever expanding belly and says, *My, my, Miss Mary Anne, you shore am a breedin' woman.*

While preparing food for the evening meal, Eula becomes conspiratorial. *I have a secret, Miss Mary Anne. Promise you won't ever tell,* she whispers.

I promise, I whisper back.

She pulls the front of her dress down far enough for me to see where her chest has never been exposed to the sun. *I am as light as you are,* she says. We both giggle over the truth of her secret.

~~~

Finally, on April 25, Richard takes me to the hospital. Because I am a medical rarity, everyone in the hospital stops by to see me. Nurses from every floor take a peek at my freaky contractions, even the lab techs stop by for a brief visit.

Put the damned stop watch down, Richard and start charging admission, I tell him.

About 2:30 in the morning of April 26, I am delivered of a nine pound boy.

Some women will do anything for a three day vacation, I tell the doctor.

~~~

Eula arrives at my home by seven in the morning every morning. She stays until her husband picks her up around five o'clock in the afternoon.

One late afternoon, after Eula has gone home, the doorbell rings. It is the neighbor Sally, who fired her maid because she asked for some of the refrigerated water being given the dog.

Sally refuses my invitation to come into the house.

After much reluctance, she informs me that I must not let that colored woman use my bathroom as she is too dirty.

This solves the riddle as to why Eula always takes the bottle of Clorox with her when using the facilities. I now understand the mystery of the toilet in the car port.

When I explain that someone who is too dirty to use my bathroom is also too dirty to wash my dishes, Sally leaves.

No neighbor visits me again.

~ ~ ~

Trees are dying in Zilker Park because of the severity of the drought. We call a tree surgeon to look at the four gorgeous sycamores that live in our front yard. He drills some holes in the ground to help water get to the roots. He is not optimistic that the trees will survive.

~ ~ ~

To teach school, I must have five years of residency in Texas before applying for a teaching credential. My naturalization papers don't count.

~ ~ ~

Cockroaches! No one seems to mind sharing their residence with these survivors of the age of dinosaurs. Except me. Once a month I take the drawers out of dressers, turn them upside down, then vacuum the crevices where cockroach eggs might lurk. Next, I scrub hidden spots in closets and kitchen corners. Grocery bags come into the house just long enough for me to unpack them, and then I take them outside for storage. It seems roaches like the paste that holds the sacks together. No foodstuff sits out on the kitchen counters and trash cans get emptied every night. To no avail.

Some genius develops a special light bulb with a slight recession in the top. After all foodstuffs are wrapped in airtight containers, all doors and drawers opened, the light bulb is screwed into a lamp, the lamp turned on. We lock all doors and windows so that no one can gain entry while the pill dissolves in the heat of the light bulb sending its poisonous fumes throughout the house, thus destroying the cockroaches. Finally, Richard drops the little white pill in the recessed top after the kids and I leave. Four hours later we return, throw open doors and windows. The last task is to sweep up the dead and dying roaches. We perform this little ritual once a month. After six months, the body count lessens but we never return to a bugless house.

Our activities amuse our wiser neighbors.

~~~

How would you feel about leaving Texas to go to California? Richard asks one night in June after he returns from work.

Like the Israelites when Moses said he was leading them out of Egypt, I reply.

How about San Diego? he asks.

I have heard of San Diego. In another life, I had dated a Marine who had gone there for boot camp.

Where are you going? he asks.

To pack, I tell him.

My joy is short lived. We do not pack up and leave until the end of October. Finally, when some burly furniture movers arrive, I suggest they be mostly careful with the china as some of it came west in a covered wagon. The china arrives in San Diego intact. The furniture does not.

~~~

We leave Austin, Texas for San Diego, California on October 26, 1956 in a no longer spiffy Studebaker. We have packed the back seat with clothes, household linens, toys, Jamie, Carla, and Max. John, six months old, and I ride shotgun.

Four tornadoes skip across the northern Texas horizon as we drive away.

No neighbor comes out to wave good-bye.

~ ~ ~

Part 6:
The Funerals

In late June 2000, Richard's health continues its slow decline. He has been to many doctors, two neurologists among them. Not until July 17 does he have an appointment with yet another neurologist. I abandon him to the care of our daughter, Carla. I am going with my sister, Barbara, to Kane for the only reunion ever held to honor that prairie hamlet. It has been sixty years since I last visited that little hamlet in southern Manitoba.

~~~

Midmorning Barbara stops the car on the shoulder of a back highway of western South Dakota for a cigarette break. I contemplate the cemetery silence. Cigarette finished. Barbara refuses my offer to drive. Now retired, she still knows these roads like the back of her hand. This was her territory when she was West River TB control nurse.

Having left Rapid City just in time to witness a late June sunrise, we speed through what once was cattle country. Many old ranchers' children and grandchildren have opted for a less rigorous life in the city as a result of the Department of Agriculture Land Bank program. We spot just enough cattle to know the region is not entirely bereft of living creatures.

As we sip the last decent cup of coffee from our thermos, we discuss the possibilities of who we might still know at the Kane reunion. I wonder if Artie Thiessen will be there. I wonder whether, if he is there, will we recognize each other? I wonder how the reunion committee ever found Barbara.

Barbara has no answers for these puzzling queries.

~~~

About noon, she pulls off the highway and drives through a small park that protects the dying town from the road. The park had been developed many years ago when Macintosh needed protection from a road that actually carried traffic.

Even trains no longer travel through here.

Perched on the North Dakota border, Macintosh had depended on the Milwaukee railroad for jobs. The railhead served the entire area by taking wheat and cattle to market. The town's small businesses offered the ranchers and farmers a variety of store-bought goods and essential commodities, delivered to their stores by the railroad.

Education beyond the state-mandated eighth grade was possible in Macintosh. The children on the Standing Rock reservation experienced an educational system strongly influenced by the Roman Catholic Church.

Carl Eskelson taught math at the Mackintosh high school where he also served as superintendent of schools. He married Madge Shirey, the elementary school's prettiest teacher. In this windblown, treeless, drought stricken, outpost, they raised three sons and two daughters. Richard, their second son, grew up to marry me after he graduated from South Dakota State School of Mines and Technology.

Two churches, one Lutheran, one Presbyterian, completed the town's ensemble. The reservation received spiritual comfort from the Roman Catholic Church.

Today, when we drive into Macintosh, the community seems uninhabited except for a house that boasts a hair salon sign from one of its curtained downstairs windows. Across the empty street a flashing neon sign announces Café Bud Light. Barbara parks and we go inside. We find one lone drunk seated at the bar, eyeing the amount left in his Pabst Blue Ribbon beer bottle each time he takes a swig. The empty dance hall silently sits behind a closed door adjacent to the kitchen. The kitchen seems as devoid of activity as the dance hall. Finally, after about forty-five minutes, the waitress-cook, an older lady who seems to be suffering from the same confusion as the man at the bar, takes our order. She delivers our brunch in the form of two cold fried eggs topped with an equally cold slice of Velveeta cheese, sans coffee. She explains the high school homecoming dance ended a few hours earlier.

Because many ranchers and farmers have left the land, the need for towns like Macintosh has followed them.

After leaving a generous tip, we flee to the serenity of a highway that separates private land from Standing Rock Reservation.

~ ~ ~

Minutes into North Dakota, we see an enormous herd of bison lolling in the warmth of a late June afternoon. Calves lie partially hidden in grass belly high to a cow pony. I wonder why none of these animals live on the Standing Rock side of the road.

~ ~ ~

Fewer than one hundred and fifty years ago the Plains Indians owned the bison on this lush grassland. The post-Civil War government sent hunters armed with buffalo guns into these sacred hunting grounds. The hunters soon cleared the prairie of bison herds, their carcasses left to rot in the prairie sun.

With the food supply slaughtered, the Lakota ageless way of life died. The army herded the remnants of tribes onto reservations.

Railroads and banks were finally free to settle this wilderness with cheap labor from northern Europe. The West was finally won.

Immigrants, lured by free land, broke sod on their ferocious new property. They plowed under the buffalo grass, planted crops of wheat, corn, flax, barley, and rye. They harvested bumper crops of wheat, corn, flax, barley, rye, and other grains. They raised hogs and poultry, and ranched beef and horses.

Now their farm buildings, houses, barns, and granaries exist only in memory. Trees planted to provide buffers against fierce prairie winds have been bulldozed. Silhouettes of rotting skeletons in huge tree bone-yards mar the prairie. Barbed wire fences and the livestock they confined have vanished taking most of the native wildlife with them. Filled ditches complete the death knell of family farming.

～～～

Before we enter the empty freeway that will take us on the eastern leg of our journey, Barbara pulls in at a rest stop for a cigarette break. The prairie wind is even-tempered today. The absence of bird song and insect buzz is stunning. *Where have all the meadowlarks gone, long time passing* I sing, dirge like, into the prairie wind. We are now well into the valley of the northern Red River.

～～～

Unhindered by traffic, we sail down the interstate until we get to the eastern edge of Jamestown where a room in a newly built Travelodge waits for us. Just before we exit the freeway, we hit rush-hour traffic. Suddenly I see a huge semi truck carrying a full load of cattle misinterpret the direction of the entrance into the motel.

I breathe all the words any cowboy would recognize into my hands as the biggest yellowiest truck in existence almost peels the paint from the passenger's side of the car.

～～～`

After this experience, I am secretly relieved that I will not be asked to drive the car for the entire 1600-mile round-trip. Something to do with being the little sister and unfamiliar with driving among cattle trucks prevents me.

～～～

At the restaurant next to the motel, our waitress takes a genuine interest in our journey and asks us if we have been to see the white buffalo. This rare animal is revered by all Plains Indians. Fences that enclose the Tatankaska flutter with written notes and bits of ribbon left in hopes the prayer requests will be granted. Before the waitress gives us directions to view the sacred Tatanka, she checks her watch, which is still set to run on farm time. Sadly the park is closed for the day, she informs us. It is not yet six o'clock.

We rise early for this last leg of our journey. We turn north to drive through the middle of the Red River Valley's incredibly rich farmlands. Here, black glacial soil produces crops that feed the world and enrich Archer Daniels Midland.

~ ~ ~

Bright miles of yellow safflower on the west side of the road and intensely blue flax on the east side of the road produce a cacophony of color Van Gogh would envy. Disregard for the soil shouts as loudly as do the colors.

~ ~ ~

We travel empty green mile after empty green mile. A new BMW zips past us. Pride of ownership has caused the proud owner to roar past us on the vacant interstate. Just to have another car on the highway amazes us and to have such a powerful vehicle rip past, inspires us. Barbara, I say, put this car in the "g" for go gear. We'll get to the border in less time.

No sooner said than a black and white North Dakota highway patrol car, concealed in the grassy meridian, zips by at an even faster speed. As we cruise past the two cars parked on the shoulder of the road, we observe the new-car owner being given a ticket by a highway patrol officer.

Any other ideas? Barbara wants to know.

~ ~ ~

Badly in need of a break from the endless emptiness of the landscape, we exit the interstate. A sign assures us that we can find gasoline and food. We fill the tank at the only gas station in Flashing, North Dakota.

Barbara and I enter the accompanying restaurant-souvenir-coffee shop and immediately order coffee. The sober waitress brings us cups of a luke warm ecru substance.

After consuming a reasonably edible lunch, we wander through the gift shop which is filled with made-in-China white bison souvenirs offerings. After a short exploration, we locate the clean but cleverly concealed restroom. The wall of my stall sports a hand lettered sign. Writ large on chartreuse Day-Glo poster board, the proclamation reads:

CONDOMS 25 CENTS

GLOW IN THE DARK CONDOMS 35 CENTS

WATCH IT GROW AND GLOW

Barbara, I whisper, *I think people here have nothing to do. Let's get the hell out of this place before someone asks us if we want to play.*

Still badly in need of caffeine, we continue our northern journey.

～～～

At the border, the Canadian immigration officer leans out of the door of his little station-house to ask if we have firearms, cigarettes or beer, the contraband most Americans smuggle into Canada. He casually waves us on our way from the doorway of his little building.

～～～

By late afternoon we arrive in Carman. Gladys, our last Canadian Auntie, has made arrangements for us to stay in a local motel. This is a businessman's outpost. Spotlessly clean, it provides few amenities.

Gladys treats us to supper in the new clubhouse on the golf course. Seated at a table window we watch golfers complete their early evening round of golf while skillfully navigating through a large flock of Canada geese.

Gladys explains that the flock does not migrate. It prefers the safety of the golf course during summer nesting season. The flock finds winter equally enjoyable because the town folk provide these large, noisy birds with a generous supply of wheat.

The 'gooshey' sections of the course seem to deter neither golfer nor goose.

~ ~ ~

We begin our first day of learning to sound Canadian again. On our way to breakfast at Gladys's house, we drive past the house Grandma and Grandpa Bruce built, where our dad and all his brothers and sisters were born, where Agnes, the twins, Grandpa Bruce, Grandma Bruce, Uncle Leash, Dad, and Aunt Mary died. The last flood destroyed its foundation. The city condemned it, and it sits emptily awaiting demolition.

~ ~ ~

After we have enjoyed lots of Glady's real coffee, she takes us on a tour of Carman.

The hospital where Barbara and I were born has been torn down along with the accompanying nurse's residence. Townhouses have taken their place, leaving no evidence that our Aunties Agnes and Helen Bruce and Auntie Edna Davidson trained there to be nurses.

The blank movie theater marquee sags under the weight of its emptiness.

The Sanders family no longer owns the drug store.

The dusty windows of Mr. Harrison's haberdashery sit empty.

The church Uncle Eddie Watson designed and built now houses a tea room bed and breakfast.

Stan Cochren no longer provides glasses for the visually impaired.

The empty train depot watches the freight trains roll past a couple of times a week. Passenger service was withdrawn long ago.

The Ryal Hotel still hugs the river's edge. Abandoned to the elements, it serves as a reminder of more vigorous days.

Even the Bank of Montreal has closed its doors.

Only the post office, Bowie's Bakery, and Doyle's Funeral Parlor remain unchanged.

The Boyne River, sluggish and green with agricultural pollutants, still wanders through town.

Where do you get your drinking water? I ask Gladys.

She explains that it comes from the river, via the treatment plant and then to us, through water pipes, just like everywhere else.

Gladys takes us shopping at the local co-op.

Aunt Mary always shopped at Safeway. While shopping, she went up and down the aisles and turned all the canned goods around so that the French labeling always faced the back of the shelf.

At the co-op, we buy Turret cigarettes for souvenirs. John Gunn always smoked Turret cigarettes. This time the change in packaging informs the potential user that:

This product causes cancer.

This product causes heart disease.

This product causes lung disease.

This product is addictive.

We ask the clerk whether she sells fewer cigarettes because of the new information. She meets our question with a curious stare in this country where one-eighth grain of codeine with Tylenol is available across the counter.

~ ~ ~

After supper we head back to our no-frills motel. Barbara wants to know whether I am worried about Richard.

No. Yes I am. He will see another neurologist about a week after I get back. None of the other doctors can understand what causes his leg tremors. They still don't know why he keeps losing weight either. He's like a bear with a sore paw, poor dear. He's had more tests than I ever knew existed. All of them have shown no abnormalities. I've lost the ability to be anxious. I'm beginning to wonder if they aren't looking for cancer. A diagnosis will be a relief for both of us. I sigh.

Next morning we prepare for the first day of the Kane reunion.

~ ~ ~

What had once been a challenging twenty-five mile drive on gravel roads is now a quick ride down a well-maintained highway. About half-way, we drive past a large abandoned farm. From here Mr. Mullins' apiary supplied us with his clover honey. We always purchased it at the now disintegrating Victorian farm house, and Barbara wasn't sure I would remember.

I do remember the perilous journey with Grandmother driving her Plymouth the twelve miles to buy gallon buckets of the clover honey that made Roy Mullins famous and rich. One year the family took a trip to Mexico. When they returned, the entire community went to the schoolhouse to watch a slide show of their journey. After we had viewed their many, many pictures, their really fat daughter, dressed in a sombrero and a serape, sang and danced something she learned in Mexico.

We arrive in Kane.

The grain elevators, unused and needing paint, stand tall against the sky as a memorial to a vanquished method of farming.

The schoolhouse where Mr. Siemens meted out stern discipline has been replaced by an empty square building.

The general store survives as a remodeled private home.

Someone dismantled the train depot, the White's house, the Cowie's house and the house that provided sanctuary for the teachers.

Even Grandfather's enormous barn, implement shed, hen house, granaries have been leveled.

The house where Grandmother enjoyed an international reputation for lavish meals and gracious hospitality has been replaced with a small, modern house.

Only a few trees of the great windbreaks remain.

Ponds and ditches have been filled to make room to produce more wheat.

No animals live on the land. No longer needed, barbed wire fences have been removed to make harvesting the last row of wheat possible.

~ ~ ~

The school yard which once offered its cindery surface for play now hosts a huge tent. Its cavernous interior houses rows of folding chairs, an excellent sound system, and a dais.

After registering and picking up our name tags, we wander through the crowd to find a place to sit in the rapidly filling tent. We see no familiar faces as the tent fills to overflowing. English, spoken with lightly accented Low German, provides familiar sounds. The program begins by recognizing each member of the reunion committee; they have earned the solid applause they receive. Neither Barbara nor I recognize any member of the committee.

Roll call begins. Barbara and I are introduced. Health reasons prevent Martha Cowie of the pony bucking contest days to attend the reunion. Health reasons also prevent Gladys Fredrickson of the cops and robbers days from attending.

I recognize no one. I finally realize I am probably seeing the children who bear the names of people I remember.

We lunch al fresco. The prairie air blows cool and sweet this Dominion Day.

Barbara and I decide to leave. The rest of the program doesn't hold our interest and we want to explore the countryside. We drive empty mile after empty mile on a new, well maintained empty highway. Prairie hen, killdeer, and meadowlark have ceased to exist here because new high-tech machinery harvests the grain up to and including the roadside cover. Nothing disturbs the monotone grain crop on the level floor of the valley. Not a sprig of wild mustard, buttercups, tiger lilies, or brambles of prairie roses gives respite from the green only landscape.

~ ~ ~

We stop for another cigarette break. The sepulchral silence overpowers us. A crop duster, making low passes over the open fields breaks the silence as it completes its contribution to loss of habitat. No crickets count the temperature. Grasshoppers no longer edit the grain fields.

~ ~ ~

Only sighing wheat remembers scent of bison, softly weeping Cree, Ojibwa, Assiniboine; labor of men and women who wrested pride of ownership from this hostile wilderness, changing it into fine farms, fine houses, fine communities in the Red River's Edenic valley.

The wheat remembers the silent footfall of those stalwart Mennonites, who, when forced to leave Imperial Russia, took their peace seeking ways with them, and packed up their worldly possessions. They sewed their precious red durum wheat into linings of trousers, long skirts, children's pockets. They found asylum in Canada, where the ancestry of their contraband enriched newly plowed grasslands, making Canada one of the world's six wheat families.

Gone, all gone, all thrown away in pursuit of higher grain production for the gaping maw of mechanized farming.

~ ~ ~

On the return to Kane for dinner, Barbara breathes deeply.

Don't you miss the smell of this air? she asks.

No. No, I miss the smell of the ocean. I feel weepy.

How can you be homesick here? she wonders.

Because here no longer exists, I tell her.

~ ~ ~

On our way to the dinner table, still bright with light at this northern latitude, an old lady comes up to me. Putting her arms around me in a tight hug, she softly asks if I remember her.

I remember you, she says. *I was a grade ahead of you. You were so cute. I knew when you moved away I would never see you again in this world, and here you are. I'm Hilda Giesbrecht.*

I return her hug.

Of course I remember you, Hilda, I lie.

She smiles in relief.

She joins us at the table and tells of her father taking her out of school after she turned sixteen because she had enough schooling for a girl. Even though her husband didn't think much of schooling either, all their children enjoy fine educations. They live close by in Winkler. The family is making arrangements for Isaac, her Down syndrome child, to be placed in an assisted living home. Hilda is getting too old to care for him full time. She is content with this decision.

Frank, one of Hilda's brothers, announces, *It's getting late, time to go home.* In answer to our question, *Where have all the farm buildings gone?* He explains that two men can farm about 10,000 acres. *No need for anyone to live on the land*, he says.

With dinner over, Hilda and Frank head south, home to Winkler. The sun, low on the horizon, still shines with amazing light at 8:30 p.m. Barbara and I head west into the low riding sun. We look forward to getting back to Kane tomorrow and the ceremonial unveiling of the cairn.

~ ~ ~

I wonder where the committee located enough rocks in this black clay soil after the latest glacier scrapped all rocks as far away as Texas. Had I known, I would have brought a big rock from San Diego and another one from Rapid City. Carman lacks rocks, too.

~ ~ ~

After a leisurely breakfast with Gladys and her never-empty coffee pot, we head back to Kane still amazed at the ease and speed the new highway provides. We sail past the World War I memorial still standing guard over Rolland. A little farther down the road we comment on how the big white church in Myrtle's dying community needs paint. With tongue in cheek, Barbara wonders if her music teacher still lives.

~ ~ ~

Once again, the committee provides us with everything. Lots of steaming hot coffee accompanies tables laden with food for a light brunch.

~ ~ ~

Barbara spies Tommy White. He seems surprised to see us. We find a place to sit and visit with him. He decided to drive the fifty miles from Winnipeg for the cairn's unveiling. *No big deal anymore*, he says.

Somehow he knows that our brother Jim has died.

He gives us a rundown on his family, our long ago favorite playmates.

Alex, eldest of the six, still lives in Roland.

Margaret enjoys her retirement from nursing. She, too, had survived a childhood appendectomy.

Frank and I celebrated the same birthdates. Older than I, he never seemed to notice my baby crush on him. No one in the family hears from him. He lives back East somewhere.

Lilly, the freckled giggly one, died many years ago.

Jean, the baby and the White family favorite, lives in Calgary.

Tommy lives in Winnipeg. He really hasn't kept up with anyone from Kane.

~ ~ ~

Too soon, time for the final gathering in the tent has arrived. Hilda and her brother find us, and the five of us find a place where we can sit together.

~ ~ ~

A spirited prairie wind tests both the PA system and the tent. Inside the protection of the full to capacity tent, a committee member reads the opening prayer. Reverend Groening recounts struggles and hardships citing difficulties in providing an educational opportunity through the 1930s. He pays honor to the dead of World War II. Because Mennonites are pacifists, the number of those young men who defied parents and church to serve their adopted country speaks of a different courage. We sing sad hymns of loss, sometimes in German, sometimes in English.

~ ~ ~

Barbara and I drift from the tent for the unveiling of the cairn, still curious as to the location of any rocks.

It is here by the veiled memorial, an older member of the committee speaks with solemnity into the microphone. In spite of the wind, he announces clearly, *As of this day, the community of Kane no longer exists. No mail will ever be received here. No new map will be marked with its name ever again.* He pulls the cord to uncover the cairn. The canvas falls away to reveal a monolith of polished black granite.

~ ~ ~

My throat constricts. When I am finally able to grab a breath of soothing, prairie air, I take Barbara's arm. *God Almighty,* I whisper, *we're at a funeral.* Her reply is a well placed kick to my ankle.

The great, black polished granite tombstone rejects future tossing of stones in remembrance of past greatnesses. The lovely engraving on the highly polished side of the marker facing the highway explains how Mr. Kane's name came to grace this once viable community. To complete the monument that faces away from the road, a dated and accurate engraving of the old school house will remind a passer-by of the length of time this building served the community of Kane.

Tommy White picks up a piece of gravel from the roadside and chucks it at the gravestone. No one notices.

~~~

Of the more than 250 people at the reunion, only Tommy White and Hilda Giesbrecht recognize us.

No one asks about Grandmother and Grandfather Davidson. Certainly no one ever heard of our Dad, Doug Bruce. That no one seems to remember Mother's and John Gunn's famous secret love affair provides us with a sense of relief.

~~~

With the reunion book, *Kane The Spirit Lives On*, firmly in hand, I hug Hilda a truly final good-bye. I realize that the cairn's rocks of memory live within all those people who took time to organize the reunion. Some rocks are far flung, firmly anchored in British Colombia, Alberta, Ontario, Minneapolis, Rapid City, and San Diego. The spirit of a tough, resilient, and caring community has taken root all over the North American continent.

~~~

And I am going home, back to where home really is, and where Richard's date with small cell lung cancer will provide a different kind of funeral for me.

~~~

Marion Eskelson

No longer do I search for what never was nor what never will be. Today I sit, sun glazed, sipping coffee, knowing the ocean will always be there, even in the dark.

Author's bio

Born in 1929 just in time to welcome the collapse of the world's economy, the author lived on her grandfather's wheat farm on the Canadian side of the north Red River valley. The day she celebrated her tenth birthday Canada declared war on The Axis powers. That same year her mother took her three children to live in Rapid City, South Dakota, United States of America, forever. In 1951 she was graduated from Yankton College, moved to Texas to marry Richard Eskelson on Bastille Day in Fort Worth. Richard, Marion, and their children moved to San Diego, California in 1956. Still residing in the much remodeled home purchased in 1957, Marion now lives happily forever after in San Diego surrounded by children, grandchildren and great-grandchildren.